Go-Carts, Catapults & Midnight Feasts

Go-Carts, Catapults & Midnight Feasts

101 Vintage Pastimes for Modern Kids

CATHERINE COX

The History Press

It is advised that children undertaking the activities featured in this book are supervised by a responsible adult at all times to ensure that no accidents occur.

First published 2015

The History Press
The Mill, Brimscombe Port
Stroud, Gloucestershire, GL5 2QG
www.thehistorypress.co.uk

British Library Cataloguing in Publication Data.
A catalogue record for this book is available from the British Library.

ISBN 978 0 7509 6429 6

Typesetting and origination by The History Press
Printed and bound in Malta, by Melita Press.

For Philip and all his friends

Contents

OUTDOOR & ADVENTUROUS

ART & CRAFT

RAINY DAY

SCIENCE & NATURE

Outdoor &
Adventurous

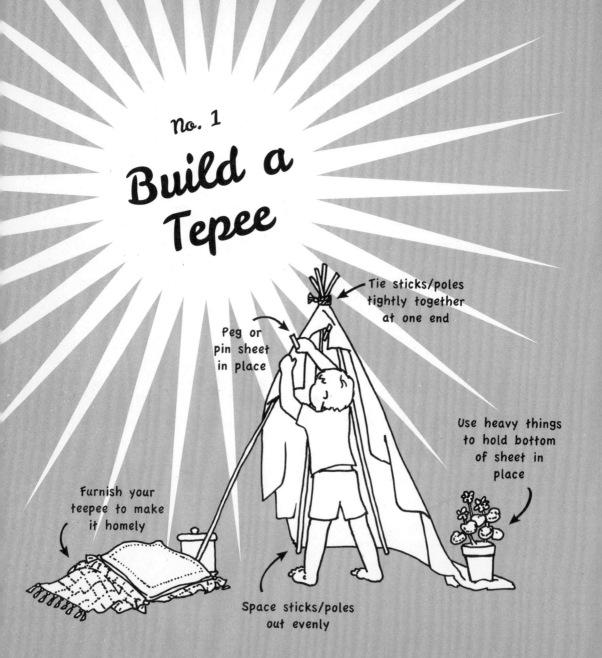

No. 1
Build a Tepee

Tie sticks/poles tightly together at one end

Peg or pin sheet in place

Use heavy things to hold bottom of sheet in place

Furnish your teepee to make it homely

Space sticks/poles out evenly

Tepees were traditionally used by Native Americans and they were designed to be easy to move from one place to another as the tribe moved. Native Americans also strapped babies to cradle boards to make them portable, but it is probably best that you don't try that. Proper tepees were covered in animal skins and had smoke flaps to let out the smoke from a cooking fire.

YOU WILL NEED

- Five beanpoles or long sticks that are at least as tall as you

- String

- Old blankets or sheets

- Pegs

IMPORTANT

DO NOT light a fire inside your tepee. It will go badly for you.

METHOD

1. Place the poles on the ground so that they are parallel to each other.

2. Tie one end of the poles together tightly (wrap the string round a few times and pull it tight before you tie a knot).

3. Stand the poles upright so that the tied end is at the top and separate out the legs. Now you have the frame for your tepee.

4. Drape your blankets or sheets around the beanpoles and peg them into place. Make sure you leave a doorway to get in!

5. Use rugs and cushions to make your tepee homely.

DATE COMPLETED   AGE WHEN COMPLETED   SIGNED

------------------------   ------------------------   ------------------------

Jumping in a pile of leaves is an essential rite of passage.
Jumps can be as simple or as complex as you like, but once you have
mastered the basics, you may as well experiment with different forms of jump.
Have a person standing by with a camera to record your best efforts.

YOU WILL NEED

- A pile of leaves (usually found under trees in parks and woods)

METHOD

1. Run up.

2. Jump.

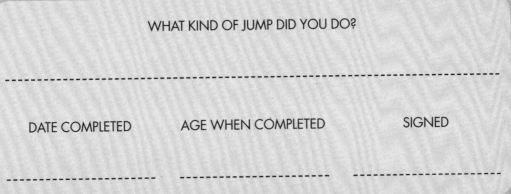

WHAT KIND OF JUMP DID YOU DO?

DATE COMPLETED   AGE WHEN COMPLETED   SIGNED

--------------------   ----------------------   ----------------------

No. 3

Have a Scavenger Hunt

A scavenger hunt is basically a treasure hunt, and it works best if you have teams or individuals competing to find the same things on the list. See who can find the most things in an hour.

YOU WILL NEED

- Pencil
- Paper
- Bag

OR

- A camera

METHOD

1. Write a list of things to find (or use the list here).
2. Divide into teams and compete to see which team can find all the things first.

VARIATIONS

If you have a camera, you could take pictures of things rather than actually 'scavenge' them. This means you could include different types of things on your list. You could have a special beach scavenger hunt.

EXAMPLE LIST

- Feather
- Round stone (or striped stone/heart-shaped stone/ flat stone etc.)
- A purple flower
- A piece of sheep's wool
- A piece of wood with lichen on it
- An oak leaf
- A conker/pine cone/acorn
- A snail's shell

WHAT WAS THE BEST THING YOU FOUND?

DATE COMPLETED   AGE WHEN COMPLETED   SIGNED

-------------------   -------------------   -------------------

no. 4

Pick Blackberries

People have eaten blackberries for at least the last 8,000 years.
During the First World War children were given time off school to collect blackberries
so that blackberry juice could be sent to the soldiers fighting in the trenches.

YOU WILL NEED

- A container to hold the blackberries (a box or bowl with a lid is much better than a bag so they don't get squashed)

- (Optional) a long stick/ walking stick to enable you to get the just-out-of-reach blackberries

METHOD

1. Find a bramble bush.

2. Pick blackberries.

3. Remove prickles from fingers.

4. Eat blackberries.

HANDY HINT

Avoid blackberries near roads as they will be dusty and avoid any blackberries below knee height if you are picking them in a place where dogs are walked.

WHAT TO DO NEXT

Blackberries are delicious raw but can also be turned into blackberry jam, blackberry crumble or blackberry ice cream. Blackberry crumble is easy to make and it doesn't matter if you don't get the measurements exactly right so if you are new to cooking try this recipe first. Blackberry jam and blackberry ice cream are a bit more difficult to make but well worth a try. You should be able to find recipes easily either in a recipe book or on the Internet.

DATE COMPLETED   AGE WHEN COMPLETED   SIGNED

------------------------   ------------------------   ------------------------

no. 5

Have a Midnight Feast

No childhood is complete without at least one midnight feast.

YOU WILL NEED

- Alarm clock

- Food

METHOD

There are two ways to have a midnight feast: one way is to plan ahead and make a picnic the evening before; the other is to sneak downstairs and raid the larder and the fridge, if your parents don't object.

If you choose the first option, then pack a basket full of exciting food. You can also include a tablecloth and plates for a really ceremonial midnight feast. Music (if it won't disturb people) could also add to the atmosphere.

If you choose the second option, then you have to make do with whatever you find.

HANDY HINT

Midnight feasts are no fun if you are cold. Snuggly jumpers, thick socks and dressing gowns make it much more fun. Taking your duvet with you is also an option, but eating in bed is not advised unless you like sleeping on biscuit crumbs.

In summer, outdoor midnight feasts can be great fun, but you would need a responsible adult with you.

WHAT FOOD DID YOU HAVE?

DATE COMPLETED   AGE WHEN COMPLETED   SIGNED

----------------------   ------------------------   ------------------------

No. 6

Learn to Skim a Stone

Send a stone dancing across the water in defiance of gravity! If you get really good, you can even challenge the world record (an unbelievable 88 skips, apparently) or enter a stone-skimming competition. Stone skimming can be a serious business; in 2010 mathematicians at University College, London published their research into investigating the mathematics of stone skimming.

YOU WILL NEED

- Lots of smooth, flat stones

- A calm river or lake (fast-flowing water is no good for learning)

- A lot of patience

METHOD

1. Hold the stone between your thumb and finger (see picture).

2. Throw it with a flick of the wrist so that the stone is spinning as it leaves your hand.

3. Aim to hit the water at an angle of 10–20 degrees.

4. Repeat until your stone bunny-hops across the surface of the water.

RANDOM FACT

Stone skimming is also called 'ducks and drakes'.

HOW MANY SKIPS DID YOU GET?

DATE COMPLETED   AGE WHEN COMPLETED   SIGNED

----------------------   ----------------------   ----------------------

no. 7

Roll Down a Hill

The first time you try this, pick a gentle slope.
It is surprising how fast you can go.

YOU WILL NEED

- A hill

- Yourself

METHOD

1. Find a slope that doesn't have rocks, thistles or trees in the way.

2. Lie along the top of the slope and stretch your arms up above your head.

3. Roll gently down.

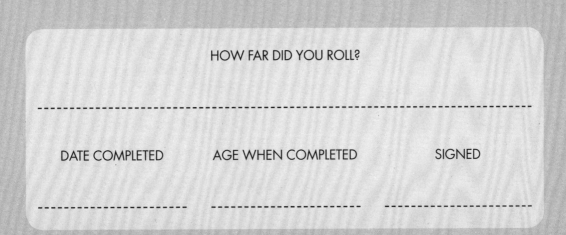

HOW FAR DID YOU ROLL?

DATE COMPLETED   AGE WHEN COMPLETED   SIGNED

-------------------------   -------------------------   -------------------------

Have an Easter Egg Hunt

It has been claimed that Easter egg hunts date back to the Protestant Reformer Martin Luther who hid them at Easter as a symbol of the Resurrection (eggs look dead, but lead to life). Easter egg hunts are usually done outside, but it is perfectly permissible to have an indoor hunt instead.

YOU WILL NEED

- Eggs (or sweets)
- Baskets/bags

METHOD

1. Hide the eggs.
2. Search for the eggs.

HANDY HINT

Unless you want your hunt to be very, very easy you should probably make sure that stages 1 and 2 are done by different people.

Count the eggs before you hide them so you know how many you are looking for.

HOW MANY EGGS DID YOU FIND?

DATE COMPLETED   AGE WHEN COMPLETED   SIGNED

No. 9

Organise a Silly Sports Day

The silly races are always the most fun races on school sports day, so why not have a sports day made up entirely of the silly ones?

YOU WILL NEED

The equipment that you choose will depend upon the events you devise. You will probably also want to provide prizes.

TYPE OF RACE	EQUIPMENT
Dressing up	Lots of clothes. Make sure that each person has the same amount of clothes to put on and that they have similar types of things – e.g. each person could have hat, jumper, trousers, shoes, belt, gloves and necklace.
Egg-and-spoon	Eggs (hardboiled if you want to avoid mess) and spoons.
Three-legged	Something to tie legs together; crepe bandage is good (and can then be used to treat the injured afterwards).
Wheelbarrow	Nothing.
Hockey ball dribble	Hockey stick (or something that could be used as a hockey stick) and ball.
Obstacle	Whatever you have to hand; blankets, chairs, beanpoles, cones etc. can all be used.
Balloon relay	Balloons.

DATE COMPLETED   AGE WHEN COMPLETED   SIGNED

----------------------   ----------------------   ----------------------

No. 10

Build a Fire and Cook on it

Food cooked on a campfire, despite its tendency to be burnt and covered in ash, always tastes better than food cooked in an oven.

YOU WILL NEED

- Dry wood
- Matches
- A bucket of water
- Food to cook
- (Optional) paper/firelighter
- A responsible adult

HANDY HINT

Make sure your woodpile is not too close to the fire.

METHOD

1. Make sure you have a responsible adult with you to help.

2. Choose a safe place to have your fire. There must not be overhanging trees, dry grass, tree roots or anything else that could catch fire accidentally.

3. Fill a bucket with water and put it close by in case you need to put the fire out in a hurry.

4. Collect wood. You will need more than you think and you need to get a lot of very dry small twigs to get the fire started.

5. Lay out a few reasonable-sized twigs or sticks next to each other to form a flat base.

6. Place two sticks parallel to each other and two more on top of those to make a square.

7. Put the firelighter (if you are using it) in the centre of the square. You shouldn't need to use the lighter though; dry moss, tiny little twigs, silver birch bark (don't take it from living trees), wood shavings and dry leaves make good 'punk' for starting fires.

8. Place the very little twigs on top of the sticks and then place slightly bigger twigs on top of that. It is traditional to build these layers up in a little pyramid/wigwam shape.

9. Light the punk/firelighter. If the fire needs help, bend down to the side of the fire and blow firmly and steadily into the middle of the fire. You should be blowing parallel to the ground.

10. Once the fire is lit, regularly add sticks and logs but be careful not to make the fire too big. You only need a small fire for cooking.

WHAT TO COOK

Once you have lit your fire, you need to decide what to cook on it. A good cooking fire is one that is full of burning embers, but not many flames. If you try to cook on flames, you will burn the outside of the food and the inside will stay uncooked.

SAUSAGES

Cook in a frying pan for at least 15 minutes and ensure that they are cooked all the way through before you eat them. Make sure the pan is old. It will never be the same again! However, you can make it easier to clean by smearing the outside with washing-up liquid before you begin to cook, then all the soot comes off easily.

BANANAS WITH CHOCOLATE FLAKE

Split the bananas open, put a chocolate flake in the middles and wrap in foil. Cook in the embers for about 15 minutes.

DAMPER BREAD

Make a basic bread dough (1 cup of self-raising flour, 1 tablespoon of butter, ½ a cup of milk, a pinch of salt). Peel the end of a thick stick to remove the bark. Make sure that it is a fresh stick so that it doesn't burn and make sure that it is from a non-poisonous tree, so that it doesn't poison you. Wrap the dough around the end of the stick and then hold it over the fire, turning occasionally. When it turns golden brown and is hard when you tap it, take it off the stick, split it open and eat with butter and jam.

PIZZA

As an alternative to dampers, you can make calzone pizzas. Flatten out a piece of dough and cover it with tomato paste, grated cheese and what ever else you fancy. Fold it in half and seal the edges by pinching them together. Wrap the whole lot in a couple of layers of silver foil and lay it on the embers to cook. Depending upon the heat of the fire, each side will take five to ten minutes. You can tell when the dough is done by tapping it to see when it feels hard. Of course you can fill your 'pizza' with anything you like. Banana and jam works well …

JACKET POTATOES

Wrap them in two layers of silver foil and cook them in the embers. They will take about an hour and a half.

SOUP

You can also cook soup over a fire. The easy way to do this is buy it ready-made, empty the contents into a pan and warm it up over the fire (choose a cool-ish bit of fire or the soup will burn to the bottom of the pan). Ideally, you want to heat it up in a cauldron with a handle so that you can hang it over the fire (you'll need to have or make a tripod to do this) but you could also use an old saucepan and sit it directly on or near the embers. Make sure you don't choose a saucepan with a plastic handle (it will melt) or that you particularly care about (you will probably wreck it). Also, never put anything galvanized on a fire, unless you want to breathe in poisonous fumes.

If you don't have a suitable pan, it is possible to make one with a clean, empty tin and some wire to make a handle. You can even just open a tin and sit the tin itself on the embers. NEVER, EVER put an unopened tin on the fire. The air inside will heat up and it will explode, sending very sharp shrapnel flying out in all directions. Metal shards lodged in your soft tissue will hurt, a lot.

CAMPFIRE SONGS

When you have had enough of cooking, you could sit around the fire, toast marshmallows and sing camp fire songs.

IMPORTANT

Try to let the fire burn out completely so that there are no big lumps of half-burnt wood when you leave. Before you go, make sure the embers are completely out by pouring water over the fire. It would be a shame to burn down your parents' garden shed or ancient woodland.

WHAT DID YOU EAT?

DATE COMPLETED   AGE WHEN COMPLETED   SIGNED

----------------   ----------------   ----------------

No. 11

Organise a Street or Garden Party

Traditionally, people held street parties to celebrate public holidays or royal events. St George (the English patron saint) has his feast day on 23 April. St Andrew (Scotland) is 30 November, St David (Wales) is 1 March and St Patrick (Ireland) is 17 March. You could also have a garden party to celebrate the start of the school holidays or a birthday.

YOU WILL NEED

- A suitable street or garden (garden is probably safer!)

- Bunting (those little flags on string)

- Balloons

- Food/refreshments

- Guests

- Games

METHOD

1. Choose the day in advance and decide on a theme.

2. Send out invitations. Make sure you tell people when and where.

3. Decide what food/drink to serve. If you are going for a patriotic saint's day, then you might like to serve traditional food and drink and decorate the garden with national flags/a national colour scheme.

4. Make your decorations. Bunting is easy to make; staple or tape coloured triangles to long lengths of string. You can also sew them on if you have a sewing machine (sewing by hand takes too long!).

5. Make your own costume.

6. Blow up balloons.

7. Prepare the food.

8. Have fun.

WHAT WAS YOUR STREET PARTY FOR?   WHAT DID YOU EAT?

------------------------------------   ------------------------------------

DATE COMPLETED   AGE WHEN COMPLETED   SIGNED

------------------------   ------------------------   ------------------------

No. 12

Make a Sandcastle or a Boat and Sit in it

I'm sure you will have built sandcastles before but have you built one big enough to sit in? The tradition of building sandcastles dates back at least to the sixteenth century, probably earlier. Today the art of sand sculpture is a very serious business with festivals and competitions held across the world. The Guinness world record for the tallest sandcastle is currently held by Caterpillar Inc who built a 12.59m tall castle in Rio de Janiero, Brazil.

YOU WILL NEED

- Lots of sand (needs to be damp or it won't stick together)

- Spade

METHOD

1. Decide whether you want a castle or a boat.

2. Choose a spot with damp sand. If the tide is coming in, make sure you are far enough up the beach to give yourselves time to finish!

3. Get digging.

VARIATIONS

SEA FORTRESS

- If the tide is coming in, build a defensive wall facing the sea. A C-shaped wall is best.

- Sit behind it as the tide comes in.

- Get soaked when it finally collapses.

DRIBBLE CASTLE

- You can use very wet sand to make a 'dribble castle' (less disgusting than it sounds). Take a handful of very wet sand and let it drip slowly out of your fingers. You can build up layers of dribbled sand into a castle shape. See who can build the prettiest castle.

DATE COMPLETED	AGE WHEN COMPLETED	SIGNED
-----------------------	-----------------------	-----------------------

No. 13

Build a Snow Animal

Instead of the usual snowman, why not be more creative next time it snows and build a snow animal instead? It's probably best to choose a simple but easily recognisable animal to start with, such as a snow owl or snow tortoise.

YOU WILL NEED

- Snow

- Spade

- Sticks/stones to make eyes and whiskers etc.

METHOD

1. Choose what animal you want to make.

2. Make it.

HANDY HINT

It is best to have your animal sitting or lying down, as snow legs are rarely strong enough to support snow bodies.

WHAT ANIMAL DID YOU MAKE?

DATE COMPLETED   AGE WHEN COMPLETED   SIGNED

----------------------   ----------------------   ----------------------

John Joseph invented roller skates in Belgium in 1760 and ever since then, generations of children have skinned their knees and grazed their hands learning to skate. His skates were based on an ice skate and had all the wheels in line. It wasn't until nearly a hundred years later that someone thought it might be easier to put the wheels on the corners instead. Those good at roller skating can do all sorts of clever things on them, like dancing or playing hockey. Interesting fact: the lamppost was invented solely to enable inept roller-skaters to stop. Ok, that may not be true, but they are definitely useful for that.

YOU WILL NEED

- Roller skates

- A helmet

- Ideally, padding. Elbow pads, knee pads etc. A strategically placed cushion might be helpful too

METHOD

1. Put on skates.

2. Wobble and fall over a lot until you get the hang of it.

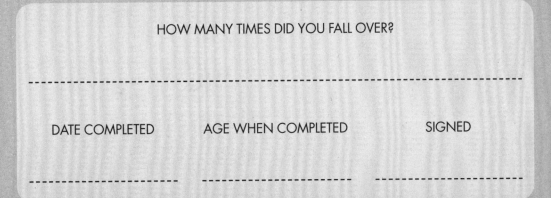

HOW MANY TIMES DID YOU FALL OVER?

DATE COMPLETED   AGE WHEN COMPLETED   SIGNED

----------------------   ----------------------   ----------------------

No. 15

Play Cricket on the Beach

Beach cricket has all the beauty of the international game, combined with additional challenges like incoming tides and other people picnicking in the outfield. You will need to adapt the rules to suit your particular 'pitch'. Many international batsmen and bowlers have honed their skills on a stretch of wet sand. For a few years between 2006 and 2009 there was even an international beach cricket series. In 2007, England won.

YOU WILL NEED

- Bat

- Ball

- Wicket
  (or anything to aim at)

METHOD

1. Divide into teams.

2. Make sure everyone agrees about the rules (such as what counts as a boundary).

3. Play game.

4. Don't forget to stop for tea at some point.

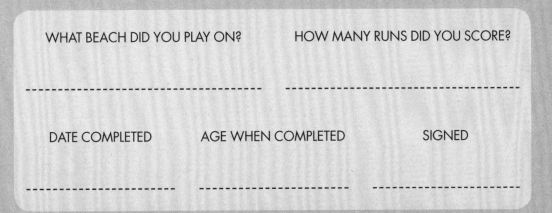

WHAT BEACH DID YOU PLAY ON?　　　HOW MANY RUNS DID YOU SCORE?

-------------------------------------　-------------------------------------

DATE COMPLETED　　　AGE WHEN COMPLETED　　　SIGNED

-------------------------　-------------------------　-------------------------

No. 16

Set a Trail for Someone to Follow

Nowadays people 'follow' each other on Twitter and Facebook. This way is much more fun.

YOU WILL NEED

- Chalk, small sticks or leaves

- A friend to try out your trail

- (Optional) a small prize to place at the end of your trail

METHOD

1. Choose a suitable place to mark out your route; woodland is probably the best place or a large garden if you are lucky enough to have one, but anywhere quiet where there are not too many people and little traffic will be fine.

2. Choose how to make your markers. The best way is to make an arrow out of leaves or sticks or draw one on the ground or trees using a piece of chalk to indicate the way you have gone.

3. Set off on your route making sure that you leave a marker every time you turn left or right.

4. If you like, you could leave a small prize at the end of your trail.

5. Take your friend to the point you started your trail and see if they can successfully follow the arrows.

WHO FOLLOWED YOUR TRAIL?   WHERE DID IT LEAD?

-----------------------------------   ---------------------------------------

DATE COMPLETED   AGE WHEN COMPLETED   SIGNED

-----------------------   ----------------------   ----------------------

Make a Bow and Arrow

It is said that it used to be a legal requirement in England that all men under 40 should practise their archery every week. In 2010 a vicar in Wiltshire used the law to call up her parishioners for archery practise. Obviously you cannot shoot without a bow. Traditionally, English longbows were made of yew wood, but any springy wood will do.

YOU WILL NEED

- A springy stick

- String

- A penknife/saw

- Firm and straight sticks to make arrows

- A responsible adult to help you

IMPORTANT

Before you fire the arrow make sure that you are not aiming at anything that would be damaged if hit (people, animals, cars, greenhouses, windows etc.).

METHOD

1. Choose a stick that has been recently cut from the tree so that it is still green. You want a stick that you can bend, but don't use something that is too thin or it won't be strong enough to make the arrow go very far.

2. Cut a small notch about 2cm from each end.

3. Tie one end of the string around one end of the stick. The string should lie in the notch that you cut in the stick.

4. Bend the stick and tie the other end of the string around the other end of the bent stick. Again, make sure that the string sits in the notch.

5. Cut a notch across the end of the firm straight sticks. These are going to be your arrows.

6. To fire your bow, hold the bow in your left hand (assuming you are right-handed) and stretch your arm out in front of you. Take one of your arrows and place the notched end in the string. Rest the other end of the arrow over the top of your left hand. Hold on to the arrow and the string with the first two fingers of your right hand, pull back and let go.

DATE COMPLETED   AGE WHEN COMPLETED   SIGNED

-----------------------   -----------------------   -----------------------

No. 18

Fly a Kite

Kite flying is another pastime that people have enjoyed for hundreds, if not thousands, of years. However, it was not always just good-natured fun. In the eighteenth century Benjamin Franklin supposedly flew a kite in a thunder storm (don't try this; it is a stupid idea). To be fair to him, we don't know if he actually did it himself, or if he just suggested it. In parts of Asia, people fight with kites, competing to slice each other's kites out of the air.

YOU WILL NEED

- A kite – you can buy one, or make your own

- A steady breeze

- A field with no power lines that the kite could get tangled in

METHOD

1. If there are two of you, one person holds the kite and the other person holds the string. Walk away from each other until there are about 20m between you. The string should be fairly tight. The person holding the kite should then throw it up into the air and the person holding the string should pull down on the string.

2. If you are flying a kite on your own then you need to unwind some of the string and then run along dragging the kite behind you until the wind catches it.

THE COLOUR OF MY KITE IS

HOW WINDY WAS IT?

DATE COMPLETED

AGE WHEN COMPLETED

SIGNED

No. 19
Learn to Use a Map and Compass

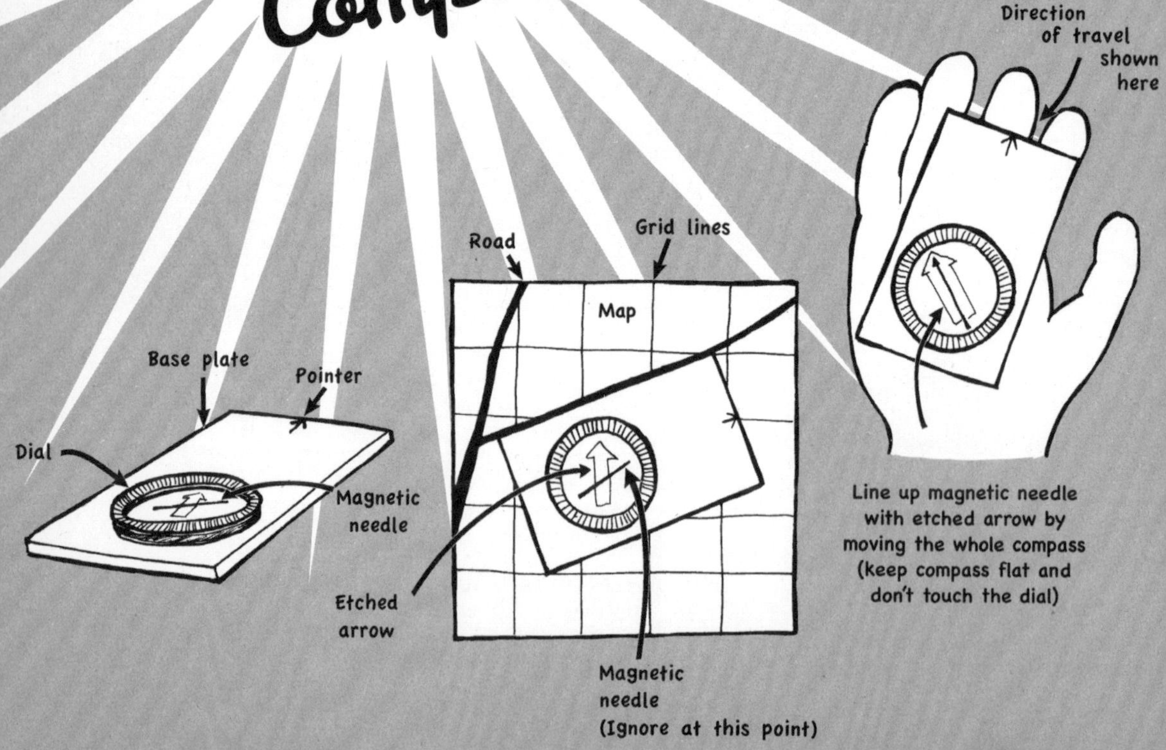

Direction of travel shown here

Base plate

Pointer

Dial

Magnetic needle

Etched arrow

Road

Grid lines

Map

Magnetic needle (Ignore at this point)

Line up magnetic needle with etched arrow by moving the whole compass (keep compass flat and don't touch the dial)

Being able to use a map and a compass is one of the fundamental skills for any budding survival expert.

YOU WILL NEED

- Map (an Explorer series Ordnance Survey map would be best)

- A walker's compass with a transparent back

METHOD

1. Before you start, look at the diagram and make sure that you know what the different parts of the compass are.

2. First make sure that you can find north. Lay the compass flat on your hand and wait for the needle to stop shaking.

3. Now you need to learn how to measure a bearing. Line the edge of the compass base plate along the path or road that you want to walk.

4. Turn the central dial of the compass round until the arrow that is drawn on the dial lines up with the north lines on the map.

5. Take the compass off the map and place it flat on your hand.

6. Turn your whole self around until the spinning arrow lines up with the drawn arrow.

7. The base plate of the compass is now pointing in the direction (bearing) of the path. Walk the way the base plate arrow points.

Once you have learned to follow a compass, have a look at the other symbols on a map and use a key to find out what they mean.

DATE COMPLETED	AGE WHEN COMPLETED	SIGNED
-----------------------	-----------------------	-----------------------

No. 20

Climb
a Tree

Tree climbing can be dangerous but so long as you are sensible about it and don't climb too high or on branches that are too thin it can be great fun. It is also a useful skill to learn as it might one day save your life – Charles II is said to have escaped the pursuing Roundheads after his defeat at the Battle of Worcester by hiding in an oak tree.

YOU WILL NEED

- A sturdy tree with low branches

- Friends (don't climb trees on your own)

METHOD

1. Make sure that you choose a tree that is strong enough to take your weight.

2. Climb it. Don't step on any dead branches. Getting up is always easier than getting down so don't go too high.

VARIATIONS

Find a tree that is comfortable to sit in. Take a book and an apple up the tree and read in peace. You might like to rig up a basket on a rope to pull things up into the tree.

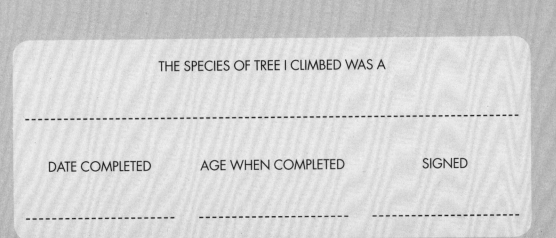

THE SPECIES OF TREE I CLIMBED WAS A

DATE COMPLETED   AGE WHEN COMPLETED   SIGNED

-----------------------   -----------------------   -----------------------

No. 21

Blindfolded 'Follow the String'

If you're ingenious you could play this game indoors,
but it is much better as an outdoor activity.

YOU WILL NEED

- A ball of string

- Blindfolds

- A place with trees, bushes or other obstacles

METHOD

1. One person sets the course. Tie one end of the string to a fixed point and then use the string to set a course through the trees. You can take it over low branches and between forked trunks so that the person following it will have to climb over and under things.

2. Blindfold everyone else. Take them to the start of the string. They should put one hand on the string and follow the course.

3. For the sake of safety, you might want to have one non-blindfolded person helping to guide them.

VARIATIONS

Have teams compete to see who can follow the course the fastest.

DATE COMPLETED   AGE WHEN COMPLETED   SIGNED

----------------------   ----------------------   ----------------------

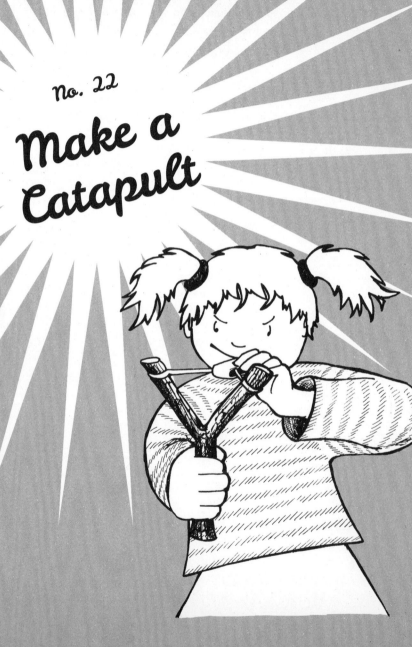

no. 22

Make a Catapult

A catapult is a device for hurling things (from the Greek *kata*, meaning down, and *pallein*, meaning hurl) and they come in all shapes and sizes. Start small now and work up to something bigger later. One day you might be able to make your own trebuchet and storm a castle.

YOU WILL NEED

- A sturdy forked stick

- Saw

- Piece of elastic

- Folded pieces of paper (for missiles)

- A responsible adult to supervise

METHOD

1. Find a sturdy stick that is forked so that it is Y-shaped. Choose a stick that is thick enough (approximately 2cm in diameter) to be strong and make sure that it is not rotten.

2. Trim the forked sections so that they are both approximately 10cm.

3. Wrap one end of the elastic around one of the fork branches about 2cm from the end and tie a firm knot.

4. Pull the elastic tight across the 'Y' and tie it around the other forked branch and trim off any excess elastic.

5. Place a folded piece of paper in the middle of the elastic, pull back and release it and see how far your missile flies.

HOW FAR DID YOUR MISSILE GO?

DATE COMPLETED   AGE WHEN COMPLETED   SIGNED

----------------------   ----------------------   ----------------------

No. 23

Go Sledging

In some countries sledging can form part of an essential way of getting around. Here it is really only done for fun, though if you want to take it more seriously you could have a sledging race. The first international sledging competition was held in Davos in Switzerland in 1883 and was won by a student called George Robertson.

YOU WILL NEED

- Snow

- Sledge (it is possible to sledge on a couple of thick binbags if you don't have a sledge, but it is not as safe and you should only go down gentle slopes)

- Warm clothes

- Hill

METHOD

1. Find a suitable hill (i.e. one without wild animals, trees in the way, rocks, roads or barbed-wire fences).

2. Take the sledge to the top of the hill.

3. Sledge down.

4. Repeat until wet and cold.

5. Go home for hot chocolate.

VARIATIONS

Can be combined with a snowball fight or making a snow animal.

DATE COMPLETED   AGE WHEN COMPLETED   SIGNED

-----------------------   -----------------------   -----------------------

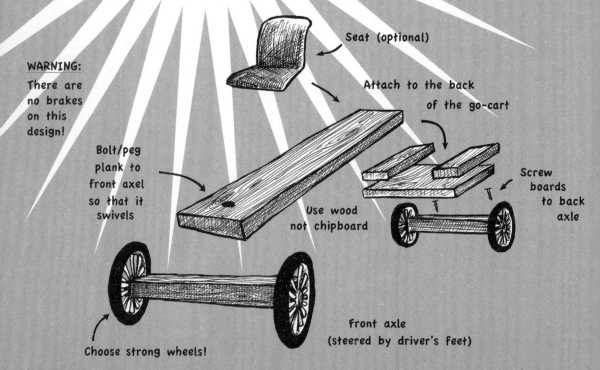

no. 24

Make a Go-Cart or Box Car

Seat (optional)

WARNING:
There are no brakes on this design!

Attach to the back of the go-cart

Bolt/peg plank to front axel so that it swivels

Use wood not chipboard

Screw boards to back axle

Choose strong wheels!

Front axle (steered by driver's feet)

Go-carts have been built for generations and are known by many different names – go-cart, box car, gravity car, soapbox. They were popularised by the American Soapbox Derby craze of the 1950s and '60s. Go-carts come in all shapes and sizes and can be built out of whatever you have to hand.

YOU WILL NEED

- Wheels are essential

- Tools (hammer, saw, nails, screws)

- Wood

- String/rope

- A responsible adult to supervise

METHOD

1. Design your go-cart before you start to make it. The most important thing is to work out how to attach the wheels. Have a look at the illustration for a rough design.

2. Make your go-cart.

WHAT DOES YOUR GO-CART LOOK LIKE?

DATE COMPLETED   AGE WHEN COMPLETED   SIGNED

-----------------------   -----------------------   -----------------------

No. 25

Spot Shapes in the Clouds

Ok, so this is an unashamedly lazy activity. Never mind – just enjoy it and let your imagination run wild. If you want to make it more technical, you can try and learn the names of different types of clouds too, but that might spoil the fun.

YOU WILL NEED

- Somewhere comfortable to lie on your back
- Clouds

METHOD

1. Lie on your back on the grass.
2. Daydream and watch the sky.

VARIATIONS

Combine cloud-spotting with going for a walk. You could use the shapes in the clouds as a basis for a story or a poem.

HANDY HINT

Make sure you are not looking towards the sun; if the clouds suddenly cleared you could damage your eyes if you were looking directly at the sun.

THE MOST INTERESTING CLOUD I SAW WAS SHAPED LIKE A

DATE COMPLETED   AGE WHEN COMPLETED   SIGNED

-----------------------   -----------------------   -----------------------

No. 26

Invent a New Ball Game

Some people say that golf was invented in Scotland by shepherds hitting stones down rabbit holes with their crooks and that rugby was invented by a schoolboy who decided to pick up a football and run with it. So, with a bit of imagination, you might invent the latest sporting craze.

YOU WILL NEED

- A ball

- Whatever else your game demands

METHOD

1. Get creative. Decide how points are scored, what moves are allowed and how many people can play. Choose a pitch/play area (you can be very creative with this) and decide upon the rules.

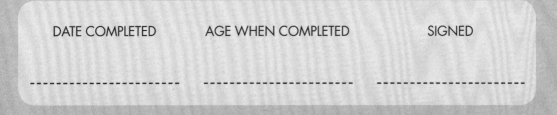

DATE COMPLETED   AGE WHEN COMPLETED   SIGNED

------------------------   ------------------------   ------------------------

No. 27

Balloon Release/ Message in a Bottle

Christopher Columbus, on his return voyage after discovering America, threw a casket in the sea containing details of his discovery after his ship got caught in a severe storm. He hoped that even if he did not survive, his report of his discovery would. In the event, Columbus survived the storm and his message was never found so it is not the most reliable form of communication but that doesn't mean that you shouldn't try it.

YOU WILL NEED

- Either a bottle with a tight-fitting lid or a balloon

- A piece of paper

- A pen

- A piece of string

METHOD

1. Write a message on the piece of paper. Make sure you include your contact details so that if a person finds it, they can phone/ write/email to tell you.

2. Tie the message to a balloon or put it in a bottle. If you are putting it in a bottle, you need to do the lid up very tightly. You might want to add duct tape over the top of the lid to help waterproof it.

3. Throw the bottle into the sea or release the balloon from a hill.

THE PLACE I RELEASED MY MESSAGE WAS

DATE COMPLETED   AGE WHEN COMPLETED   SIGNED

-----------------------   -------------------------   ------------------------

No. 28

Bury a Time Capsule in the Garden

Time capsules are a great way to keep a record of the things that are important to you. You can either bury one and leave it, in the hope that someone in the future will find it, or you can bury one with the intention of digging it up in a few years time to remind you of how things used to be.

YOU WILL NEED

- A container with a tight lid

- Plastic bag without holes

- Duct tape

- Whatever you want to put in your time capsule

METHOD

1. Decide what you want to go into the capsule. Newspaper clippings, photographs, a letter, a CD of music, things personal to you would all be good choices.

2. Put the contents of your time capsule in the plastic bag first and tie a knot in it (if any water gets in, it will ruin the things you have buried).

3. Put it in the container, fix the lid on tightly and then use the duct tape to tape tightly over the join (again, to stop water getting in).

4. Bury it and make a note of where you have put it. If you have made a map of the garden, you could mark the position on the map.

THE THINGS IN MY TIME CAPSULE ARE
DATE TO OPEN MY TIME CAPSULE

DATE COMPLETED
AGE WHEN COMPLETED
SIGNED

No. 29

Make a Survival Shelter and Sleep in it

Survival shelters can take many different forms and shapes.
This is one of the simpler designs.

YOU WILL NEED

- A long strong branch

- Lots of shorter lengths of wood

- A tree with a fork (or somewhere to rest one end of the shelter)

- A lot of leaves

- A sleeping bag

- A groundsheet to keep the creepycrawlies at bay

- Friends (don't sleep outside on your own)

METHOD

1. Choose a piece of flat, dry ground in a sheltered place.

2. Securely wedge one end of the long branch in the crook of a tree. Make sure it is a strong branch; you don't want the shelter to collapse on you in the night.

3. Lay lengths of wood diagonally up against the long branch. They need to be close together, with no gaps.

4. Once all the wood is in place, cover the shelter with leaves. The leaves are your insulation and you need a deep layer of them to keep you warm. You should create a layer of leaves that is as deep as your finger-tips to your elbow.

5. Put a thick layer of leaves inside the shelter to act as a mattress.

6. Find something to cover the entrance, or build a mound of leaves to give you some shelter.

THE PLACE WHERE WE MADE OUR SHELTER WAS

DATE COMPLETED   AGE WHEN COMPLETED   SIGNED

-----------------------   ----------------------   -----------------------

no. 30

Dam a Stream

Building a simple dam out of stones is comparatively easy and very satisfying. Unless you are highly skilled in engineering your dam will be washed away within a few hours so you will only be causing a temporary change. However, beavers are capable of changing whole landscapes with their sophisticated dams. Don't emulate them; causing floods is bad.

YOU WILL NEED

- A shallow stream

- A lot of stones

METHOD

1. Choose the point of the stream that you want to dam. A narrow-ish spot is usually best.

2. Build a wall of stones across the stream.

3. See if you can create a calm pool upstream of the dam and pick a spot for a dramatic waterfall.

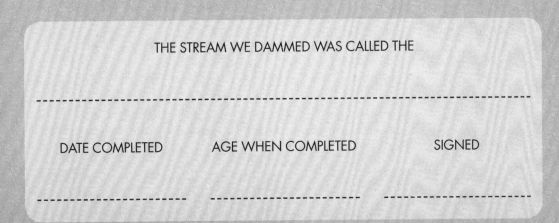

THE STREAM WE DAMMED WAS CALLED THE

DATE COMPLETED   AGE WHEN COMPLETED   SIGNED

-----------------   -----------------------   ------------------------

No. 31

Play
Pooh Sticks

The game pooh sticks originates from A.A. Milne's book *A House at Pooh Corner*. Since the 1980s Pooh Sticks Championships have taken place in the UK.

YOU WILL NEED

- A bridge

- A stream

- Sticks

METHOD

1. Find a stick that you will be able to identify as yours.

2. Stand on the upstream side of a bridge and watch the water flow under it. Try to identify the bit where it is flowing fastest.

3. On a count of three (any number would do, but three is conventional) drop your sticks together.

4. Race to the other side of the bridge and see whose stick comes through first.

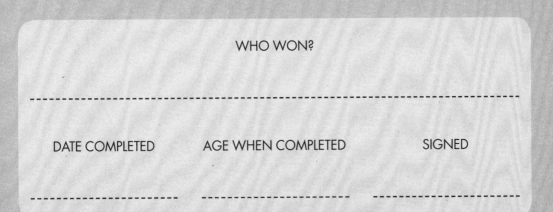

WHO WON?

- -

DATE COMPLETED   AGE WHEN COMPLETED   SIGNED

- - - - - - - - - - - - - - -   - - - - - - - - - - - - - - -   - - - - - - - - - - - - - - -

Set up a Sculpture Trail in the Garden

SPIRAL

Anything can count as art, if you look at it the right way, so putting together a sculpture trail is easy. You might even be able to earn yourself a bit of extra pocket money by charging people to view it.

YOU WILL NEED

- Something to make your sculptures from. See what is around. Flowerpots, stones, pot plants, bits of old bicycle; anything that looks arty.

METHOD

1. Build your sculptures.

2. Write a label for each exhibit.

3. Invite people round to view it.

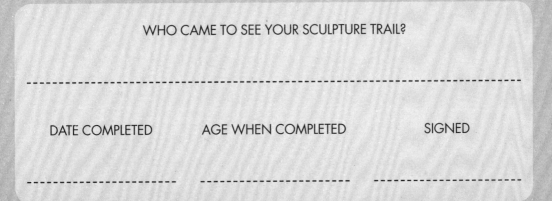

WHO CAME TO SEE YOUR SCULPTURE TRAIL?

DATE COMPLETED   AGE WHEN COMPLETED   SIGNED

----------------------   ----------------------   ----------------------

Make up a Morris Dance

Morris dancing is a traditional form of country dancing done in England.
Many dances use props like sticks, garlands or handkerchiefs.
If you are not sure what morris dancing is, see if you can find
a video of it on the Internet to see what it should look like.

YOU WILL NEED

- A minimum of four people (including you) but six is a better number

- Music (ideally traditional morris tunes)

- (Optional) sticks/handkerchiefs

- (Optional) bells tied to your shoes

METHOD

There are several basic morris moves that you might like to incorporate. Put some music on and have fun.

- STAR: Put your right hands into the middle and walk/skip around clockwise for eight beats of the music. Swap hands and go anticlockwise for eight beats.

- MARCH: Basically walk/skip forward for eight beats and then walk/skip backwards again.

- DO-SI-DO: Face a partner, walk forwards passing right shoulder to right shoulder. With your backs to each other, take a step to the right and then walk backwards so that you are back to your starting position.

- SPIN YOUR PARTNER: Hold hands with your partner and spin on the spot.

- HITTING STICKS: (Ok, so I don't know what it is actually called.) Take your stick and bang it a couple of times on the ground. Then hit your partner's stick a couple of times (be careful not to hit them). Repeat.

- SHOUTING: A lot of morris dances also involve loud war-like shouts at key moments of the dance. Be loud.

Once you have invented a couple of dances, you need to perform in front of an audience.

DATE COMPLETED	AGE WHEN COMPLETED	SIGNED
-----------------------	-----------------------	-----------------------

Art &

Craft

no. 34

Make a Collage

A collage is a picture made by gluing different materials to a piece of paper. The word comes from the French *'coller'*, which means 'to glue'. According to the American painter Robert Motherwell, 'Collage is the twentieth century's greatest innovation.' Presumably he didn't rate space rockets, computers, or Einstein's theory of relativity very highly.

YOU WILL NEED

- Collage bits (scraps of paper, magazine pictures, food packaging labels, old Christmas cards, fabric scraps, pasta shapes, dried lentils and peas, small pebbles, stones or shells, dried leaves and pressed flowers etc.)

- Glue

- Paper

- (Optional) scissors

METHOD

1. Take your piece of paper and start gluing.

HANDY HINTS

Make sure that you choose glue that is appropriate for the type of things that you want to stick. A collage doesn't quite have the same effect if bits keep falling off it. Glue sticks will work for paper and card, PVA works for wood and some materials. If you want to stick plastic or fabric you might need to buy a special type of glue. If you use glue with a solvent in it, then make sure you use it in a well-ventilated place (i.e. open the window!).

It is often easier to draw a rough outline of your picture first, and use this as a guide for where to stick the bits.

DATE COMPLETED	AGE WHEN COMPLETED	SIGNED
----------------------	----------------------	----------------------

no. 35

Marble
Paper

The art of marbling paper is ancient. The Chinese did it first and it only became known about in Europe in the sixteenth century when Crusading knights brought back beautifully marbled papers from the Middle East. Marbled paper was often used in book binding to make a decorative feature of the inside cover. The term 'marbled' relates to its appearance as it can look like the stone called marble. Stone marble is, if you're interested, a metamorphosed limestone which basically means it is a limestone that has been sat on by a mountain until the heat and pressure cause chemical changes happen.

YOU WILL NEED

- Marbling ink/ thinned oil paint

- A large deep-sided tray or bowl filled with water

- A paint brush or a pipette (dropper)

- Old comb/fork/stick/ feather to create patterns

- Paper

- White spirit (or equivalent) to clean your brushes

METHOD

1. Put old clothes on and cover everything in sight with newspaper.

2. Fill your tray with water.

3. Use the pipette or paint brush to put splodges of colour on to the surface.

4. Use an old comb or fork or a feather to drag and swirl the colour around to make pretty patterns.

5. Lay a sheet of paper carefully on top of the water (make sure it doesn't sink).

6. Carefully grip the paper at one end and then peel it up off the water.

7. Hang up your sheet of paper to dry.

You can experiment with different ways of making patterns. Blowing the colour, rather than combing it, can create interesting effects.

DATE COMPLETED   AGE WHEN COMPLETED   SIGNED

-------------------------   -------------------------   -------------------------

Make a Paper Dart

① ② ③ ④
Fold → lines

⑤
Fold up to diagnonal crease

⑥ ⑦

⑧ Fold in half vertically + open up

⑨
Turn over and fold

⑩ Fold top back up

⑪
Fold the sides in

⑫
Fold top over

⑬

⑭ ⑮

Fold them in again

⑯
Throw 'plane

Making a paper dart is easy. Making one that actually flies is much harder. Describing how to make one is harder again. Pay attention and look at the pictures! It will make no sense without them.

YOU WILL NEED

- Paper

METHOD

1. Get an A4 piece of paper.

2. Fold the top (short) edge down to meet the long edge (should look like a triangle, with one corner cut off). Then unfold (we are making creases at the moment).

3. Repeat with the same top edge but take it down to the other long side.

4. Look at your piece of paper. You should have a nice diagonal cross at one end of your piece of paper. Got that? Good, move on to stage five.

5. Fold the right-hand long edge up to meet the diagonal line. This time, don't unfold it. Leave it there.

6. Repeat with the left-hand long edge. You should now have a sort of dart shape, but it doesn't have a pointy nose.

7. Check. Does it look like the picture? Good. Carry on.

8. Fold the whole thing in half lengthwise to get a nice long line along the middle and unfold (again, we are just putting creases in).

9. Fold it in half crosswise so that what was the top, touches the bottom.

10. You should have a triangular flap on top. Fold it back on itself about $2/3$ of the way up.

11. Fold the sides in once so that the edges follow the line of the triangle sides.

12. Fold them in again so that you now have something that resembles a volcano.

13. Fold the top of the volcano over twice.

14. Turn your volcano over and fold it in half along its length. Does it look more like a plane and less like a volcano? Good. Nearly done.

15. Fold the wings down.

16. Throw your plane. Feel triumphant.

DATE COMPLETED	AGE WHEN COMPLETED	SIGNED
-------------------------	-------------------------	-------------------------

No. 37

Write a
Short Story
or Play

A good story has interesting characters, imaginative descriptions of places and usually some type of secret or puzzle to keep the reader interested. Go and be creative. If you are struggling for inspiration you could try some of the suggestions below.

YOU WILL NEED

Well, you'll need something to write on and with, but beyond that, you don't need anything special.

METHOD

A. People watch. Choose a person and try and imagine what their life might be like. What are they doing? Why are they wherever they are? What dark secret do they have?

B. Choose an object and think about what might happen to it in the future, or what has happened to it in the past.

C. Open a book at random. Shut your eyes. Stab the page with a finger and read whatever sentence you have pointed to. That will be your first line. Run with it!

D. Reinvent a superhero version of yourself or an evil twin version of yourself and imagine what adventures you would have.

E. Go and sit somewhere quiet and start by writing about the place. Think about your senses. What can you see/touch/hear/smell? Sit in a cupboard or under a bed and use that as the start of a story.

DATE COMPLETED	AGE WHEN COMPLETED	SIGNED
-----------------------	-----------------------	-----------------------

Make a Pop-Up Book or Card

① Fold a piece of card in half

② Decorate the front

HAPPY BIRTHDAY

③ Cut out and decorate the pop-up element

④ Fold in half

⑤ Fold back tabs and glue them

⑥ Glue tabs to the inside of the card. Let one side dry before you glue the other

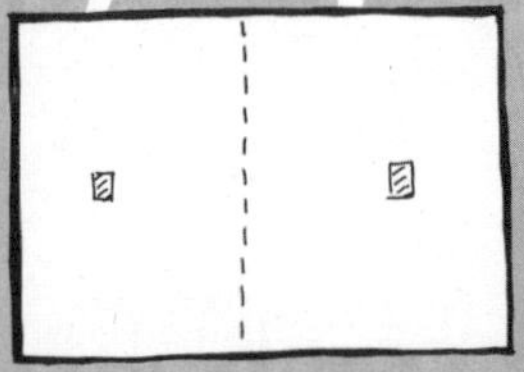

⑦ Write your message

SPLASH   To Dad

lots of love xxx

Make sure that the pop-up part does not protrude when card is closed

Pop-up books have a surprisingly long history. A Benedictine monk called Matthew Paris created a book with rotating paper discs called volvelles. His moving parts were used to work out the timing of holy days. During the nineteenth century more publishers began to use this type of technique, and by the twentieth century, pop-up books for children became common. Simple pop-up cards are easy to make.

YOU WILL NEED

- Card
- Scissors
- Glue
- Pens/paints/decorative items

METHOD

1. Make a normal card.

2. Draw whatever shape you want to pop up.

3. Add a 'tab' (a small paper hinge with which to stick it down) on each side.

4. Cut out your shape.

5. Fold it in half vertically.

6. Put glue on the tabs and stick one half to each side of the inside of your card (you will have to be patient and hold it while the glue dries).

You can also make much more complicated pop-up constructions. You could add things with tabs to pull, flaps to open or wheels to rotate.

DATE COMPLETED   AGE WHEN COMPLETED   SIGNED

------------------------   ------------------------   ------------------------

no. 39

Pyrography

Pyrography literally means 'fire-writing' and is probably one of the earliest art forms in the world. Human + fire = graffiti. If you have a special pyrography tool, called a pyrography iron, you can create very intricate decorative patterns or draw pictures in wood. However, most people probably don't have a pyrography kit at home and you don't need anything more sophisticated than a poker and a fire.

YOU WILL NEED

- Fire

- A poker

- Wood

- A bucket of water

- An oven glove or similar

- A responsible adult to supervise

METHOD

1. Heat one end of the poker up in the fire.

2. Using gloves, hold the other end <u>carefully</u>; metal is very good at heat transfer.

3. Touch the hot end to a piece of wood and hold it there until scorch marks start to appear (you should not need to press hard).

4. You will need to reheat the poker a few times because it cools down quickly.

You could try making a sign for your house with the house name and number on it. Or, if you have made a tepee, you could create a notice with your tribe name on it or (if you are unfriendly) a 'keep out' sign.

IMPORTANT

1. Be careful.

2. Have a bucket of water ready, just in case.

3. Use a thick oven glove or gardening glove to protect your hand.

4. Don't put the poker down on anything that might catch fire.

DATE COMPLETED	AGE WHEN COMPLETED	SIGNED
------------------------	------------------------	------------------------

no. 40

Make a Rubber Band Paddle Boat

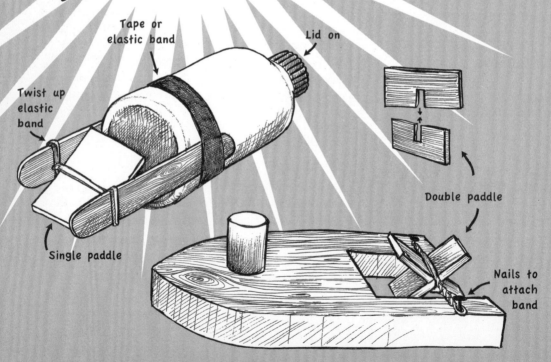

Tape or elastic band

Lid on

Twist up elastic band

Single paddle

Double paddle

Nails to attach band

A paddle boat is a boat propelled by a rotating paddle (obvious really) rather than by wind, by oar or by propeller. Human-powered paddle boats were used in China over a thousand years ago. The Romans had warship paddle boats powered by oxen. Your boat may not be quite up to going to war, but it should still move swiftly through the water.

YOU WILL NEED

You could either make this boat out of wood (if you have the relevant tools) or you could make it out of an old bottle and a couple of sticks. If you want to make it out of wood, then look at the picture and use that to make a template of your boat. If you are making the bottle version, you need the following:

- An old drinks bottle with its lid

- Two lolly sticks or wooden chopsticks (or any similar light-weight long things)

- Waterproof tape or more elastic bands

- Strong elastic band

- Stiff plastic or wood out of which to make the paddle

METHOD

1. Screw the lid on to the bottle tightly (this is the prow of your boat).

2. Fix the sticks to each side of the bottle so that they stick out behind. Use waterproof tape or elastic bands to hold them in place.

3. Put a second elastic band between the two sticks. Try to find a band that is the right size to sit comfortably between them with minimal stretch.

4. Cut a rectangle of stiff plastic or wood and slip it between the two sides of the band.

5. Wind up your paddle, put the boat in water and let go.

HANDY HINT

If you need to alter the buoyancy of your boat, you can put a bit of water into the bottle.

DATE COMPLETED	AGE WHEN COMPLETED	SIGNED
-----------------------	-----------------------	-----------------------

No. 41

Make Puppets

A well-known variant of Murphy's Law states that any pair of socks put in the washing machine will invariably emerge with one sock missing. Consequently, every household has a good supply of odd socks. Some houses even have a designated 'odd-sock drawer'. The easy availability of odd socks, combined with their range of attractive colours and bold patterns, makes them an excellent raw material for making puppets.

YOU WILL NEED

- A sock

- A hand

- Eyes/ribbons/fabric scraps

- Glue or needle and thread

- Scissors

METHOD

A very basic sock puppet can be made thus:

1. Place sock on hand.

2. Animate sock with hand.

However, most sock puppeteers would prefer to personalise their puppets. Those who are able, can sew on buttons for eyes, a felt tongue, a fluffy pom-pom Mohawk and add ribbon collars, capes and other details. Otherwise use glue to achieve a similar result (although not all glues stick fabric effectively).

Once you have made your puppets, you can stage a puppet show. A sofa is a quick and easy sock puppet stage as the puppeteer can easily hide behind it. Alternatively, a sheet hung across a washing line or beanpole can provide a similar arena. You could film your puppet show and add a commentary voice-over and special effects.

DATE COMPLETED	AGE WHEN COMPLETED	SIGNED
------------------------	------------------------	------------------------

no. 42

Plant a Miniature Garden

Creating miniaturised trees (Bonsai) and landscapes in trays (Penjing) has been popular in Asia for centuries and some miniature landscapes were believed to have magical or spiritual properties. To make a Bonsai tree takes a lot of time and skill. They must be carefully pruned to sculpt them into realistic tree shapes, and have their roots trimmed to keep them small. A tiny Bonsai tree might be decades old and will cost hundreds (if not thousands) of pounds.

YOU WILL NEED

- A tray

- Soil

- Small plants and flowers

- Rocks/stones/bits of wood and bark

- Optional extras: bits from toy farm, model railway layouts etc. to add detail

METHOD

When you are collecting plants to put in your miniature garden, you need to try to collect things with small leaves that look as if they could be miniature versions of bigger plants. Sprigs of herbs like thyme make realistic trees, alpine plants often have small leaves and moss is a good small-scale alternative to grass. You can use rocks to make miniature cliffs and caves and twigs to make fallen trees. You might like to make a gravel path or a pond out of silver foil.

If you use plants with roots, then your garden will grow (provided you remember to water it). Don't forget to take a picture of your garden once you have made it and see if you can photograph it in a way that makes it look like a real landscape.

DATE COMPLETED   AGE WHEN COMPLETED   SIGNED

-----------------------   -----------------------   -----------------------

no. 43

Map the
Garden

There are two ways of doing this: the easy way and the hard way. The easy way involves sketching out the shape of the garden and marking on key features (trees/pond etc). The harder way involves measuring it first and then drawing a plan to scale.

YOU WILL NEED

- Tape measure

- Pen

- Paper

- Another person to hold the end of the tape measure

METHOD

1. Work out the basic shape of your garden (square, oblong etc.) and draw a quick sketch.

2. Measure the width and length of the garden and draw these on the map (if your garden is an irregular shape, you might like to divide it up into simpler shapes and measure them all separately).

3. Mark key features on your map (flower beds, trees, gate).

4. Measure the position and width of the features and mark these on the map.

5. Draw a scale map by drawing everything $1/10$ of actual size. For example, if your garden is 8m wide, you would draw it 8cm wide (you can alter the scale if this seems too small). Draw the shape of your garden first and then add in the features.

Once you have a map of the garden, you can either use it as a treasure map, or you could use it to decide what you will plant where. You could even keep a garden diary over the year with maps of the different seasons showing what you have planted and harvested.

DATE COMPLETED   AGE WHEN COMPLETED   SIGNED

------------------------   -------------------------   -------------------------

no. 44

Build a Box Castle

If you don't want to build a castle, then you could make a
box aeroplane, car, submarine or lighthouse instead.

YOU WILL NEED

- Lots of boxes
- Strong scissors
- Parcel tape

METHOD

There is no set method for this; let your
imagination run wild. You could cut
castellations around the top of the walls and
include arrow slits for attacking the enemy.
You could join boxes together to make a
secret tunnel or use old cardboard tubes as
a cannon. Every castle needs a flag and you
could have fun designing your own coat of
arms. With a couple of bits of string you could
make a raiseable drawbridge to keep out
the foe.

  If you are too big to fit into the size of boxes
you have, you could still use boxes to make a
toy castle. Or you could find bigger boxes!

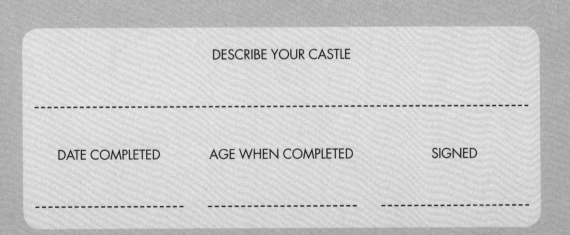

DESCRIBE YOUR CASTLE

DATE COMPLETED   AGE WHEN COMPLETED   SIGNED

----------------------   ----------------------   ----------------------

no. 45

Make a Papier Mâché Mask

The Chinese invented paper, so it is not surprising that they invented papier mâché too. Papier mâché is both light and surprisingly strong and, if it is lacquered with a tough waterproof coating to keep it dry, then it can last for a long time. Bowls, masks, boxes, furniture and even soldiers' helmets were made of papier mâché.

YOU WILL NEED

- Lots of paper

- Glue (slightly watered-down PVA is probably best. You can use flour and water paste, but if it takes too long to dry, it might go mouldy!)

- A large paint brush (to apply the glue)

- A balloon

- Vaseline

- Elastic

METHOD

1. Blow up the balloon until it is the right size for you to make your mask.

2. Spread a <u>thin</u> layer of Vaseline on the oval side of the balloon (this is to stop the paper from sticking).

3. Put a layer of paper on top of the Vaseline and then carefully spread glue on top.

4. Add another layer of paper and then another layer of glue.

5. Keep building up the layers, occasionally allowing time for the layers to dry.

6. Once you have built up at least ten layers (ideally more) leave it for a couple of days to dry out.

7. Once it is dry, remove it from the balloon, trim the ragged edges and cut two eye-holes and a couple of smaller holes at the sides for attaching some elastic so that the mask will stay on your face.

8. Decorate your mask.

Once you have mastered the art of papier mâché, think about what else you could make from it.

DATE COMPLETED   AGE WHEN COMPLETED   SIGNED

-----------------------   -----------------------   -----------------------

No. 46

Make a Periscope

PATTERN

GAP AT TOP

FRONT · LEFT · BACK · RIGHT

TOP

45° ANGLE

THIN BARS TO MAKE MIRROR SUPPORTS

BOTTOM

GAP AT BOTTOM

CUT-AWAY VIEW

Shiny side of mirror

Opening at the top

Non-shiny side of mirror

Opening to look through

A periscope is that thing on top of a submarine that peeps out of the water first. On cartoon submarines it often has a blinking eye on the end. Your periscope won't have that (at least, not unless you have some serious Frankensteinian skills) but it will enable you to see over the wall of your box castle.

Periscopes are thought to have been invented by Johannes Gutenberg in the fifteenth century, who thought that pilgrims visiting the Aix-la-Chapelle festival would be interested in buying something that would enable them to see over the crowd (apparently they weren't, and he went bankrupt). In 1854 the wonderfully named Hippolyte Marié-Davy reinvented the periscope for use in the navy. Another use for periscopes was found during the First World War as it enabled soldiers to peer over the top of the trench without getting their heads blown off.

YOU WILL NEED

- Two square mirrors

- Strong ridged cardboard (or wood)

- Something to cut the cardboard or wood

- Protractor, ruler and pencil

- Strong tape (e.g. duct tape)

- Glue

METHOD

1. Cut out four long rectangles (see picture). The exact size will depend upon the size of your mirrors.

2. Cut two squares for the top and bottom of the periscope.

3. Mark a 45-degree angle line at each end of two of the rectangles.

4. Glue some strips of cardboard either side of the line to create a slot to support the mirrors.

5. Once the glue is completely dry, tape three sides of the periscope together.

6. Slide the mirrors into place.

7. Tape the last side in place.

8. Go and look over the top of something.

DATE COMPLETED   AGE WHEN COMPLETED   SIGNED

------------------------   ------------------------   ------------------------

No. 47

Make an
Advent
Calendar

Advent is the period that leads up to Christmas. Traditionally, like Lent, it was a time of preparation and of fasting. Now it tends to be more about eating lots of chocolate. Advent calendars mark off the days in a countdown to Christmas and usually consist of a festive scene with twenty-four doors to open and chocolates hidden behind. However, there are other ways to make a calendar.

MATCHBOX CALENDAR

1. Stack up twenty-four match boxes (four rows of six would work well) and glue them together.

2. Write a number on each drawer. Mix them up to make them harder to find.

3. Use a split pin to make a handle for each drawer.

4. Wrap a strip of festive paper around the outside of all the boxes.

5. Put a sweet in each drawer.

SOCK WASHING-LINE

1. Tie up a string somewhere it won't be in the way.

2. Peg twenty-four socks to the line (baby/toddler socks would be ideal).

3. Safety-pin a number and a picture to each sock.

4. Put a sweet/tiny treat in each sock.

ADVENT CLOCK

1. Draw a clock face with twenty-four numbers written on it in order. You could put a Christmassy picture by each number too.

2. Cut a clock hand out of stiff cardboard.

3. Use a split pin to attach the hand to the clock face so that it rotates (make the pin tight enough that it does not slip).

4. Move the hand on one 'minute' each day.

DATE COMPLETED	AGE WHEN COMPLETED	SIGNED
-----------------------	-----------------------	-----------------------

no. 48

Make a Flick Book

Flick books actually work in the same way as film, by showing you a series of still images quickly enough that your brain is tricked into thinking it sees motion. Most traditional TVs update the image sixty times per second, which is fast enough to fool the human brain. However, this is not fast enough to fool dogs, and to them, TV looks like a series of flickering still images. (More modern high-definition TVs refresh faster and can fool dogs as well as humans.) Optical illusions that created movement were very popular in the nineteenth century. Some methods of viewing them were unwieldy, like the spinning Zoetrope which involved looking through the slits of a rotating drum at a set of images inside; others, like the flick book (patented in 1868 by John Barnes Libbet), were much simpler.

YOU WILL NEED

- A small notebook

- A pen

METHOD

1. Choose what story you want to tell. Pick something simple for the first time. For example, a stick man throwing and dropping a ball.

2. Draw one picture on each page. Make sure that the pictures are similar, and that each thing only moves a tiny amount each time.

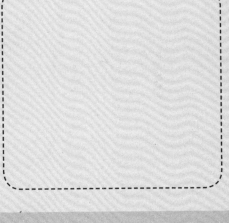

SKETCH THE FIRST PICTURE FROM YOUR FLICK BOOK HERE

DATE COMPLETED

AGE WHEN COMPLETED

SIGNED

-       -   -

No. 49

Build a Marble Run

Marbles have a long history and many ancient civilisations had a marble equivalent and their own special games to play with them. Given that marbles have been so important in human history, it is clear that they deserve fun too! Give your marbles a break from being smashed into one another and make them a marble run playground.

YOU WILL NEED

- Boxes/tubes/cardboard

- Scissors

- Glue

METHOD

The easiest way to do this is probably to use old cardboard tubes (from the inside of kitchen rolls or wrapping paper) cut in half to make 'slides', but look around the house to see what else you could find to use. Try to be creative in your marble run. You could have a trap door for the marble to fall down, a weighted seesaw, a small bucket on a string to descend in.

Once you have made a marble run, you could make a wall with different sized doorways in it. Write a score over each doorway, low numbers for wide doors, high numbers for narrow doors. Take turns to roll a marble at the doors and see who can score the highest number of points in ten turns.

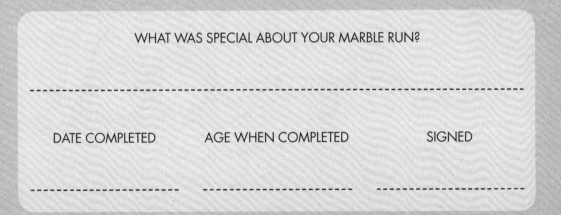

WHAT WAS SPECIAL ABOUT YOUR MARBLE RUN?

DATE COMPLETED   AGE WHEN COMPLETED   SIGNED

----------------------   ----------------------   ----------------------

no. 50

Texture Rubbings

Creating rubbings has been used by archaeologists to record the detail of stone carvings or of brass work. Sometimes, details that were hard to be seen by eye, could be made clearer in a rubbing. It used to be possible to go and make rubbings of the memorials in churches and cathedrals but this has now been stopped in case people damage the artefacts. However, there are plenty of other things around that have interesting textures that you could record by rubbing.

YOU WILL NEED

- Thin-ish paper

- Wax crayons

- Soft pencils

- Chalk

- Things of different texture (coins, stone, brick, woodgrain)

METHOD

1. Place your piece of paper over the thing that you want to make a rubbing of.

2. Gently rub the crayon to and fro in broad, consistent strokes. You might find it works best if you use the whole length of the crayon.

3. Experiment with chalk and with pencils to see which produces the best rubbing.

HANDY HINT

Stopping the paper slipping is one of the most difficult bits of taking rubbings. If possible, tape the paper down. Use masking tape so that you can remove the tape from the paper again without damaging it.

THE BEST RUBBING I DID WAS OF

DATE COMPLETED   AGE WHEN COMPLETED   SIGNED

----------------------   ----------------------   ----------------------

No. 51

Start a Newspaper

Start your own newspaper or magazine, either by yourself or as part of a group. You could make it a regular thing, or it could be a one-off.

YOU MIGHT LIKE TO INCLUDE

- News stories

- Book/film/music reviews

- Puzzles (crosswords, quizzes, children's puzzles)

- Letters page

- Agony aunt column

- Nature column

- Historical article

- Trivia

You could try starting a school magazine and get lots of different people to contribute.

MY NEWSPAPER WAS CALLED

DATE COMPLETED   AGE WHEN COMPLETED   SIGNED

----------------------   ----------------------   ----------------------

no. 52

Teach a Dog a Trick

Obviously, for this activity you need a dog. You will also need dog treats; tiny pieces of cheese or ham are 'high-value' treats that will motivate your dog very effectively. Remember, you might need to reduce the amount of food you give your dog at mealtimes if you have used a lot of treats while training them. Some dogs pick up tricks quickly, while others take a lot longer. Make sure your dog enjoys the training and don't make the training sessions too long.

METHOD

Assuming your dog already knows how to sit, you can easily teach him to shake hands.

1. First, get the dog to sit.

2. Then, take the dog's paw in your hand and shake it gently before immediately giving the dog a treat.

3. Repeat this a few times and then, once the dog has got used to it, rather than taking the dog's paw immediately, just hold your hand out. The dog may well lift its paw and offer it to you. If he does, then shake 'hands', praise the dog liberally and give him a treat.

4. If the dog doesn't offer you his paw, then you need to go back to lifting his paw yourself a few times until he gets the idea.

5. Once your dog raises his paw each time you hold your hand out, you can introduce a verbal command. For example, 'shake hands'. Say the command clearly as you hold your hand out and try to say it in the same tone of voice each time.

6. Keep rewarding the dog every time he gets it right.

7. Eventually, you should be able to get the dog to raise his paw before you hold your hand out, just by using the verbal command alone.

8. If your dog enjoys learning tricks, see what else you can teach him. You could try teaching him to go backwards, roll over or touch an object with his nose.

DATE COMPLETED   AGE WHEN COMPLETED   SIGNED

------------------------   ------------------------   ------------------------

no. 53

Design an Imaginary Fantasy Animal

All the best stories have imaginary animals in them, but it is actually surprisingly difficult to think of a completely new animal. You need nothing but your imagination to do this activity, but assuming you want to do more than just think, you will need pens, paints or craft materials to bring your animal to life. There are lots of different ways to make your animal. You could:

- Draw or paint it.

- Make a collage using pictures cut from old newspapers or magazines. You could combine bits of animals that exist but you could get much more creative by using textures from landscapes or from pictures of furniture to create interesting skin/fur/feathers.

- Make a model out of plasticine, playdough or clay.

- Use old boxes and old packaging.

- Sew a soft toy version of your imaginary animal.

Once you have designed an animal you need to come up with a name for it. You could then write a story about it or draw a cartoon strip. As an alternative, you could design an alien or create a new superhero.

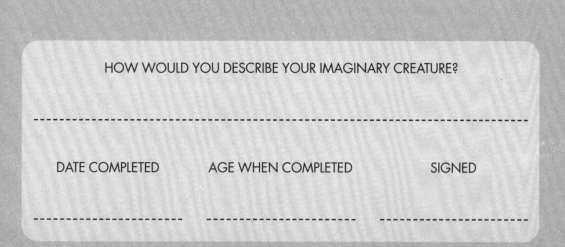

HOW WOULD YOU DESCRIBE YOUR IMAGINARY CREATURE?

DATE COMPLETED   AGE WHEN COMPLETED   SIGNED

----------------------   ----------------------   ----------------------

no. 54

Learn to Hoot Like an Owl

There is probably not a lot of point to this skill (except that you get to confuse owls), but it sounds quite impressive if you can do it well.
You could always use it as a secret call for your secret society.
If the instructions sound confusing, you might find it easier just to look at the picture.

METHOD

1. Put your thumbs together so that they are in line from top to bottom.

2. Fold the fingers of your right hand down behind your thumbs, so that your index finger is behind the joint of your thumbs.

3. Fold your left hand over round your right hand (imagine you are trying to hold a butterfly in your hands without crushing it).

4. Bend your thumbs slightly so that they are folded over your index finger.

5. Place your mouth over the joint of your thumbs and blow gently but firmly.

6. If you don't manage to make an owl sound, try moving the position of your thumbs slightly, or blow at a slightly different angle.

Your multi-functional, opposable thumbs can also be used to make seagull noises.

1. To squawk like a seagull you need to take a long blade of grass and hold it between your thumbs so that it is pulled tight.

2. It should be anchored firmly at the top (between the top of your thumbs) and at the bottom (held by the fleshy bit where your thumb turns into your hand).

3. Place your mouth against your thumbs, just below the joint, and blow. You need to blow firmly enough to make the grass vibrate, but not so hard that you break it.

4. If it doesn't work, you probably haven't stretched the grass tightly enough. It needs to be taut, otherwise it won't vibrate properly when you blow.

Seagull squawks are best used to make people jump. Creep up behind them, and do it as loudly as you can.

DATE COMPLETED	AGE WHEN COMPLETED	SIGNED
----------------------	----------------------	----------------------

No. 55

Make Sweets and Biscuits and have a Tea Party

Making homemade sweets, cakes and biscuits is easy and great fun. One of the easiest types of sweets to make are peppermint creams. Chocolate crispy cakes are also very simple.

PEPPERMINT CREAMS

YOU WILL NEED

- Icing sugar
- Water
- Peppermint essence
- Orange/lemon zest

METHOD

1. Mix icing sugar and water to make a stiff paste.
2. Add a couple of drops of peppermint essence or some grated lemon or orange rind.
3. Roll into small balls.
4. Leave them to harden.
5. Eat.

CHOCOLATE CRISPY CAKES

YOU WILL NEED

- A spoonful of butter or margarine
- Paper cases
- Rice Krispies or cornflakes
- Two Mars bars
- Chopping board
- Knife
- Saucepan
- Spoon

METHOD

1. Melt the butter in a saucepan.
2. Chop Mars bars into small pieces.
3. Add to the melted butter.
4. Melt <u>slowly</u> on a low heat. If you burn it, it won't work.
5. Stir in Rice Krispies or cornflakes.
6. Put a spoonful of mixture into each paper case.
7. Refrigerate.
8. Eat.

DATE COMPLETED	AGE WHEN COMPLETED	SIGNED
------------------------	------------------------	------------------------

no. 56

Play the Sock-Stealing Game

This is not a complicated game, and it requires no special equipment.
It is very silly but great fun to play (especially if you have a lot of people).
Warning: You may end up with carpet burns and torn socks.
Don't use socks to which you are emotionally attached.

METHOD

1. Put on socks. If you want to make the game hard, put long socks on and pull them all the way up. If you want to make it easier, wear shorter socks, and start with them already part way off your feet.

2. Kneel on the ground.

3. Every player then tries to remove everyone else's socks without losing their own.

4. The winner is the last person still wearing a sock.

You can always experiment and add new rules to vary things a bit. Try playing in teams or add in a ball and try to score a goal at the same time.

WHO WON?   WHAT COLOUR WERE THEIR SOCKS?

------------------------------------   ------------------------------------

DATE COMPLETED   AGE WHEN COMPLETED   SIGNED

----------------------   ----------------------   ----------------------

no. 57

Play the Cardboard Box Game

This is another game that requires minimal equipment.
All you need is an old box. An old cereal box is ideal but any box will do.

METHOD

1. Place the box on the ground and take turns to bend over and pick the box up with your teeth. If you fall over or put a hand on the floor, you are out.

2. Tear a strip off the box and go round again.

3. The winner is the last person 'in'.

HANDY HINT

Challenge an adult to play; you will easily beat them.

Depending on how difficult you want the game to be, you can ban players from holding on to their own knees/ankles as they bend over. It is much more difficult with the 'no bracing' rule.

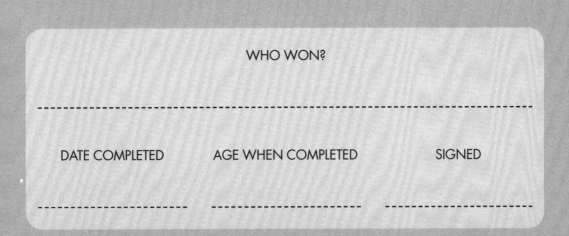

WHO WON?

DATE COMPLETED   AGE WHEN COMPLETED   SIGNED

----------------------   --------------------------   ------------------------

Set up a Secret Society

TOP SECRET

You don't need any special equipment for this.
All you need is a couple of friends and some imagination.

A SECRET SOCIETY NEEDS

- A name

- A password

- A secret code

- A secret symbol

- A secret meeting place

- A mission

One of the best things about a secret society is sending each other secret messages. There are lots of ways of doing this. Try all of the following and decide which method you like the best.

- Make up your own substitution code with different symbols for each letter.

- Write a message in lemon, apple or orange juice (lemon is best, because it leaves least colour). The message will dry invisible, but if you hold it near a heat source the acid left from the juice will turn brown and the writing will appear.

- Leave a message in a newspaper by making pin-prick holes under the letters or words that you want to form part of a message.

- Learn Morse code or Semaphore and try to send a message over a distance.

Use code or invisible ink to answer these questions:

WHAT IS THE NAME OF YOUR SOCIETY?	WHAT WAS YOUR FIRST PASSWORD?	WHO ARE THE FOUNDING MEMBERS?
-----------------------	-----------------------	-----------------------
DATE COMPLETED	AGE WHEN COMPLETED	SIGNED
-----------------------	-----------------------	-----------------------

no. 59

Play Matching Cards

This game requires the eyesight of an archer and the bravery of a rugby player.

YOU WILL NEED

- A lot of old Christmas, Easter or birthday cards

- Floor space

HANDY HINTS

Remove all shoes, jewellery or sharp objects before beginning play.

A one-way system between the box of cards and the playing area is advisable.

METHOD

1. All the cards need to be cut in half.

2. One set of halves should be spread out on the floor.

3. The other set of halves need to be in a bag or a box.

4. Each player is given a half from the box and has to find the matching half on the floor.

5. All players try to find their matching halves at the same time.

6. As soon as a half is found, that player can get another half to match.

7. The winner is the person who ends up with most pairs at the end of the game.

WHO WON?

DATE COMPLETED   AGE WHEN COMPLETED   SIGNED

------------------------   ------------------------   ------------------------

no. 60

Put on a Show

You might think that putting on a show is complicated, but it needn't be. In England, there were no purpose-built theatres before the time of Elizabeth I and groups of travelling players would journey from place to place, putting on shows in a different place each day. Most of these groups only had between four and ten people so they would have to play several parts each. All the actors would be men or boys, which explains why the romantic characters in Shakespeare's plays spent a lot of time talking about being in love and very little time actually kissing!

Of course, you don't have to perform a play, you could put on any type of show you like.

You could do any of the following:

- Put on a play
- Do a monologue

- Sing silly songs
- Sing dramatic songs
- Do impressions
- Play a musical instrument

- Do a mime
- Do a magic trick
- Tell jokes

You could make a programme for your event and create props and costumes.

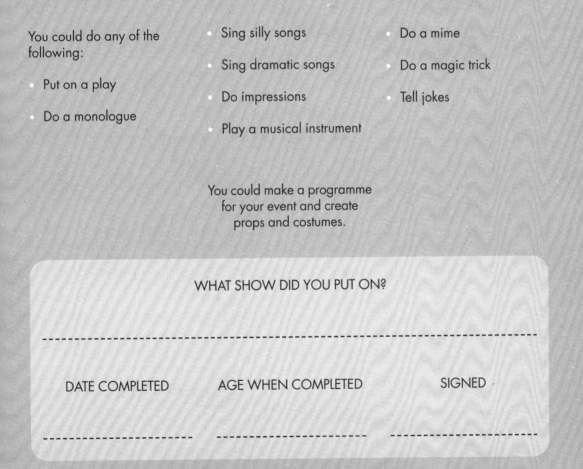

WHAT SHOW DID YOU PUT ON?

DATE COMPLETED   AGE WHEN COMPLETED   SIGNED

----------------------   ----------------------   ----------------------

No. 61

Start a Collection

A collection is anything that you deliberately have a lot of! You can make a collection out of anything, and often the fun is not so much in what you actually end up with, but the excitement of finding things that fill gaps. Choose something that interests you and that won't cost much money.

CLASSIC THINGS TO COLLECT

- Stamps
- Labels/packaging
- Fossils
- Old/unusual coins
- Postcards/birthday cards

- Sea glass (the little bits of polished glass you find on beaches)
- Shells
- Stickers
- Pictures cut from newspapers/magazines
- Autographs

Once you have a collection, you need to decide what to do with it. If you collect something flat (stamps, labels, photos etc.) then you could stick them into a scrapbook or album. If you collect fossils or coins then you might want a box or a shelf to display them.

The best-displayed collections are clearly labelled. Think about what information you might like to put with your collection. If you have a lot of collections, you can set up your own museum!

DATE COMPLETED   AGE WHEN COMPLETED   SIGNED

------------------------   ------------------------   ------------------------

no. 62

Make Your Own Lemonade

Obviously you can buy lemonade, but it is not as much fun as making your own. All you really need is sugar (usually caster sugar) and lemons. You don't even need kitchen scales. You could experiment with other citrus fruit too and make grapefruit and lime-ade.

YOU WILL NEED

- Lemons
- Sugar
- Water
- Pan
- Jug

METHOD

1. You need about half a cup of sugar to each cup of lemon juice. So squeeze your lemons and measure the amount of juice you have (it doesn't need to be exact).

2. Measure out the same amount of water as sugar and mix both together in a pan.

3. Heat up the water and the sugar and bring it gently to the boil. Stir it occasionally, but not too much.

4. Mix the sugar water syrup with the lemon juice.

5. Leave to cool.

6. Drink it.

DATE COMPLETED   AGE WHEN COMPLETED   SIGNED

------------------------   ------------------------   ------------------------

No. 63

Cut a Banana Before you Peel it

Yes, it is possible and yes, it is pointless.

YOU WILL NEED

- A banana (preferably one with a few brown speckles on it)

- A long needle

METHOD

1. Insert the (clean!) needle into the banana and rotate it round to slice through the banana inside the skin.

2. Repeat at intervals along the banana's length.

3. Replace the banana in the fruit bowl, hide and wait!

Provided that you inserted and withdrew the needle really carefully, there should be barely any mark on the skin of the banana. The person who opens it should, therefore, be very surprised when it falls into neatly sliced pieces when they peel it.

Smirk proudly and don't tell them how it is done. Now might be a good time to follow up with a vanishing-coin trick or some mind-reading to cement your reputation for wizardry.

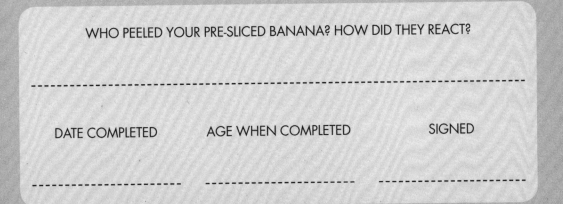

WHO PEELED YOUR PRE-SLICED BANANA? HOW DID THEY REACT?

DATE COMPLETED   AGE WHEN COMPLETED   SIGNED

----------------------   --------------------   ----------------------

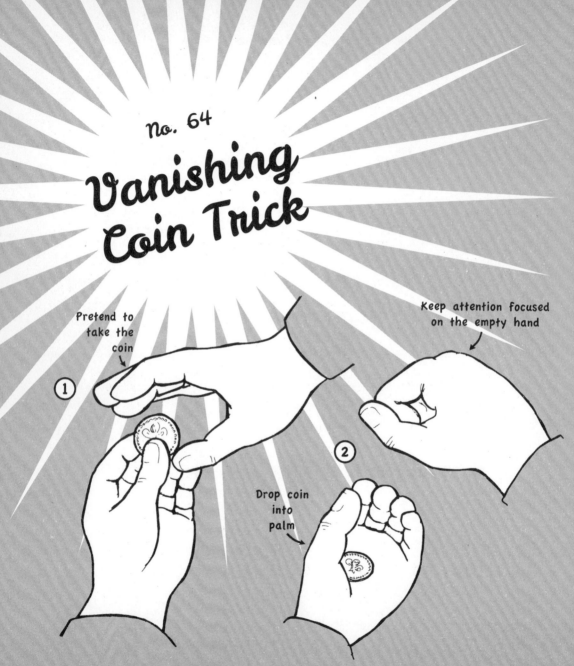

No. 64
Vanishing Coin Trick

Pretend to take the coin

1

Keep attention focused on the empty hand

2

Drop coin into palm

A lot of magic tricks need fancy equipment or take ages to learn. This is a simple sleight of hand trick that only requires a coin and a bit of practice in front of a mirror.

METHOD

1. Hold the coin in your left hand so that the coin is clearly visible to your audience. Your fingers should be towards your audience so that only you can see the palm of your hand.

2. Pretend to take the coin with your right hand. However, instead of actually taking the coin, allow it to drop into the palm of your left hand.

3. Distract your audience by closing your right hand quickly and firmly as though grasping the coin. Keep looking at your right hand, whilst allowing your left hand to drop casually to your side.

4. Invite the audience to tap your right hand.

5. Dramatically open your right hand to reveal nothing there!

HANDY HINT

No matter how much your audience pleads, <u>do not repeat the trick</u>! They will be looking to see how it is done and it will be much harder to misdirect their attention.

DATE COMPLETED	AGE WHEN COMPLETED	SIGNED
-----------------------	-----------------------	-----------------------

no. 65

Mind-Reading for Beginners

This is another simple magic trick, but for this you need a secret assistant who is in on the act. If you place your hands over your own cheeks and clench your jaw a few times you will notice that you can feel the muscles tightening. However, if you do it while standing in front of a mirror, you'll notice that the movement cannot be seen. This is the basis for this trick.

METHOD

1. Tell the audience to choose a number.

2. Leave the room and make sure you are clearly out of earshot.

3. When you return, pick out your assistant seemingly at random and stand behind them, placing your hands on the side of their head, as though you are going to read their mind. Make sure that your hands are in a position where you can feel their jaw clenching.

4. Ask your assistant to think hard of the number that the audience chose so that you can 'read it from their mind'.

5. Count the number of times your assistant clenches their jaw.

HANDY HINTS

Big numbers would take ages to do if your assistant clenched their jaw that many times. Do it in units instead. For example, seventy-four would be done by seven clenches, then a pause, followed by four clenches.

Make it look difficult. Frown, pull faces, insist on silence, hum in a spiritual way.

DATE COMPLETED	AGE WHEN COMPLETED	SIGNED
-----------------------	-----------------------	-----------------------

no. 66

Drama Challenge

There are all sorts of games you can play based around drama
and improvisation. I think this is one of the most fun.

YOU WILL NEED

- A collection of props

- Paper and pens

- At least six people

- Three bowls

METHOD

1. Each person writes down four props, two places or scenarios and four character types and places their slips of paper into the bowls (one bowl is for the props, one for the places and one for the characters).

2. Divide the group into pairs/threes. The first pair takes a scenario from the scenario bowl and each person takes a character from the character bowl and a prop.

3. The pair then have to create an improvisation based on the characters, props and scenarios that they have.

VARIATIONS

Another drama challenge is freeze-frame improvisation. It is an easy one as it requires no set up. A pair start an improvisation and carry on until someone shouts freeze. The pair freeze in position. The person who called out 'freeze' then takes the position of one of the people and the improvisation carries on, often on an entirely different line.

DATE COMPLETED	AGE WHEN COMPLETED	SIGNED
-----------------------	-----------------------	-----------------------

no. 67

Make a Surprise Present for Someone

SURPRISE

You may well have made presents before for birthday/Christmas etc. However, if you make a surprise entirely-unexpected-totally-unforeseen present the recipient will be particularly impressed by your generosity and thoughtfulness. Spread a little love with a random act of kindness. The equipment you need and the method you use obviously depend entirely on what you choose to make. Possible things could include:

- Sweets/biscuits

- A decorated photo frame

- A collage

- A poem written out and decorated

- A small bag or purse

- A recipe folder

- Wind chimes

- A knitted scarf

- A painted stone paperweight

- A toy boat or car

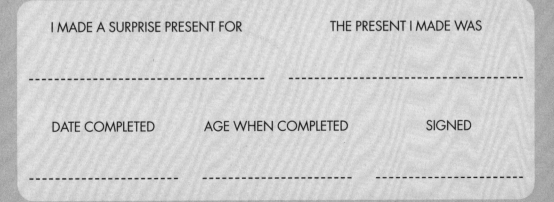

I MADE A SURPRISE PRESENT FOR   THE PRESENT I MADE WAS

------------------------------------   ------------------------------------

DATE COMPLETED   AGE WHEN COMPLETED   SIGNED

---------------------   ---------------------   ---------------------

no. 68

Play the Memory Game

This is another good game to play against adults
(the older the better). You are bound to win.

YOU WILL NEED

- A tray

- A cloth to cover the tray

- A stopwatch/clock

- A never-ending supply
  of objects

- Paper and pens for
  everyone taking part

METHOD

1. One person fills a tray
   with between fifteen and
   forty objects.

2. The players have two
   minutes to try to memorise
   everything on the tray.

3. The tray is removed and
   then everyone has to write
   down any objects they
   can remember were on it.

4. The winner is the person
   who can remember the
   most things.

HANDY HINT

Try to come up with
strategies to help you to
remember the different
objects. For example, group
them by shape (five objects
are round), by colour,
by association (six things are
to do with sport) or by who
they belong to.

WHO WON?.

DATE COMPLETED   AGE WHEN COMPLETED   SIGNED

----------------------   ----------------------   ----------------------

no. 69

Make up a Group Story

This is another of those challenges which is all about you using your own imagination, so there won't be detailed instructions.

YOU WILL NEED

- A group of friends
- Creativity

METHOD

1. Everyone sits in a circle.
2. One person starts the story off and then pauses whenever they like.
3. The next person carries on. They can say as much or as little as they like.

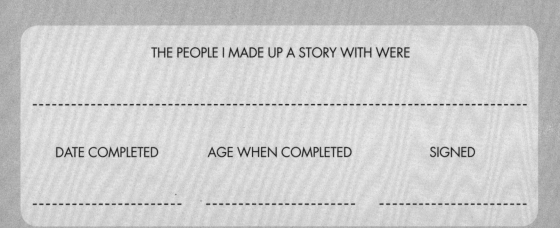

THE PEOPLE I MADE UP A STORY WITH WERE

| DATE COMPLETED | AGE WHEN COMPLETED | SIGNED |

----------------------   ------------------------   ------------------------

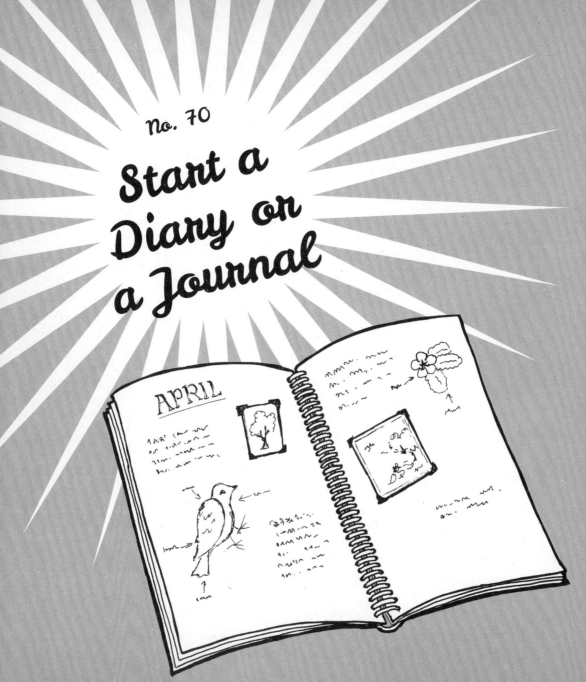

No. 70

Start a Diary or a Journal

APRIL

Keeping a diary or a journal can be a fun way to keep track of your thoughts, and it is something that you might enjoy reading back through later. You don't have to write in it every day, just whenever something interesting has happened. You could stick in photographs, letters or even newspaper cuttings. Some people draw doodles or write poems in their diaries too.

YOU WILL NEED

- A notebook (you don't need a special book to act as a diary; any notebook will do)

- A good hiding place to keep it in

METHOD

If you don't want to keep a diary all the time, then a holiday diary or scrapbook is a fun alternative. Draw maps of the walks you have done or places you have been to, make a note of the meals that you have eaten and keep leaflets or tickets from attractions that you visited. You could get all the people on holiday with you to write an entry in your journal. Stick in a few photos from the trip and you will have a lovely keepsake for the future.

HANDY HINT

You could keep parts of your diary in code if you want to make it really secret.

DATE COMPLETED   AGE WHEN COMPLETED   SIGNED

-----------------------   -----------------------   -----------------------

No. 71

Go on a Rainwalk

This is as simple as it sounds.

YOU WILL NEED

- Rain
- Waterproof clothes
- Boots
- Hot drinks for when you get back
- (Optional) waterproof camera

METHOD

1. Go for a walk.
2. Jump in puddles.
3. Take soggy pictures.
4. Come back to tea and toast.

WHO DID YOU GO ON YOUR RAINWALK WITH?

DATE COMPLETED   AGE WHEN COMPLETED   SIGNED

------------------------   -------------------------   -------------------------

Science & Nature

no. 72

Grow Crystals

Crystals come in all sorts of shapes and sizes and are formed by a process called 'nucleation', when atoms or molecules connect to each other in a regular, repeating pattern.

SALT CRYSTALS

YOU WILL NEED

- 2 teaspoons of vinegar
- 1 cup of hot water
- ¼ of a cup of salt
- A piece of sponge
- A saucer
- (Optional) food colouring

METHOD

1. Heat the water and then dissolve the salt in it. Add the vinegar.

2. Put a piece of sponge on the saucer and dot food colouring on to it.

3. Pour the solution over the sponge.

4. Put the dish somewhere warm so that the liquid can evaporate.

SUGAR CRYSTALS

YOU WILL NEED

- 1 cup of water
- 3 cups of sugar
- Glass jar
- String
- Water
- Food colouring
- A pencil

METHOD

1. Heat the water and dissolve the sugar in it.

2. Add some food colouring.

3. Pour the solution into the jar (let it cool a little first, so that it doesn't crack the jar!).

4. Tie the piece of string around the middle of the pencil and lay the pencil across the jar so that the string hangs down inside the solution.

5. Put it somewhere where it won't be disturbed and wait for a few days.

DATE COMPLETED   AGE WHEN COMPLETED   SIGNED

------------------------   ------------------------   ------------------------

no. 73

Press Leaves

Fallen leaves will decay over time but if you press them they can be preserved for several years and they can then be used to make cards or for decorations. Or you can just keep them as a collection – see if you can get a sample of a leaf from all the native trees of Britain.

YOU WILL NEED

- A flower press or heavy books

- Kitchen paper or baking paper

- Leaves

METHOD

1. Collect leaves or flowers.

2. Place them on a sheet of kitchen paper between the pages of a book. Place another piece of kitchen paper on top. The paper ensures that the leaves and flowers don't leave marks in the book.

3. Shut the book and place another couple of heavy books on top.

4. Leave undisturbed for several weeks.

5. Stick the pressed leaves in a scrapbook or use them to make cards or decorations.

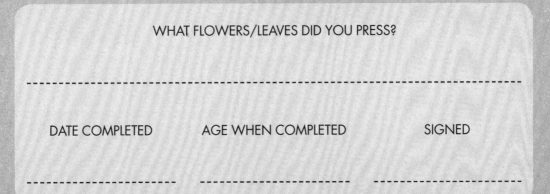

WHAT FLOWERS/LEAVES DID YOU PRESS?

DATE COMPLETED   AGE WHEN COMPLETED   SIGNED

-----------------------   ------------------------   --------------------

no. 74

Spot Orion at Night

The name 'Orion' is taken from Greek mythology. However, the constellation has been given other names by different cultures. For example, the Babylonians knew him as 'The Great Shepherd' and medieval Muslim astronomers knew him as 'The Giant'. In the northern hemisphere, you will be able to see Orion in winter and spring.

YOU WILL NEED

- A clear sky

- Night time

METHOD

1. Orion is a very easy constellation to spot as it is so distinctive. Look for the stars of the belt first. You should be able to see three stars in a diagonal line.

2. See if you can spot the stars making up his bow (to the right of the constellation) and his club (up to the left).

VARIATIONS

Once you have learned to recognise Orion, see what other constellations you can spot. If you can find the Pole Star then you will be able to find out which way is north at night. Sometimes the Earth moves through areas of sky that are full of meteorites. When this happens, you have a good chance of seeing shooting stars. Often newspapers will say if there is going to be a particularly good chance of a meteorite shower.

WHERE WERE YOU WHEN YOU SPOTTED ORION?

DATE COMPLETED   AGE WHEN COMPLETED   SIGNED

------------------   ----------------------   ----------------------

Hunt for Animal Tracks

COOT

DUCK

BADGER

Front   Back

FOX

Front   Back

HEDGEHOG

Front   Back

FALLOW DEER

MUNTJAC DEER

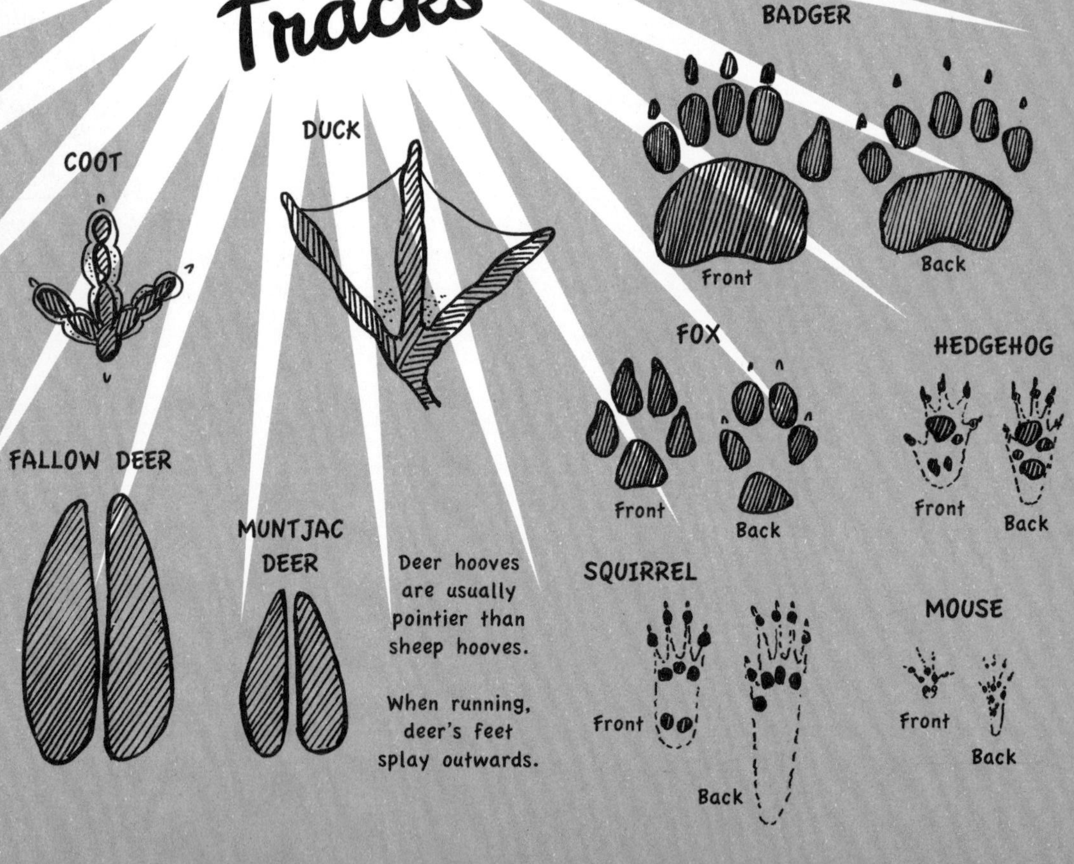

Deer hooves are usually pointier than sheep hooves.

When running, deer's feet splay outwards.

SQUIRREL

Front   Back

MOUSE

Front   Back

Identifying animal tracks is one of the oldest human skills, dating from the time when we first hunted animals for meat. Presumably our ancient ancestors would have found it useful to know whether the animal they were following was a tasty rabbit or an angry grizzly bear. You can also learn to identify animals by their poo, but footprints are less messy.

YOU WILL NEED

- Soft ground (mud or snow)

- Your own observational skills

- A guide to animal tracks (a few are pictured here, but you can look online or in natural history books to find out others)

METHOD

1. Go and be observant. As well as tracks, look out for animal hair, tunnels or pathways through the undergrowth, chewed nut or seed cases or animal droppings.

I FOUND TRACKS OF

DATE COMPLETED   AGE WHEN COMPLETED   SIGNED

-----------------------   -------------------------   -------------------------

no. 76

Keep Caterpillars

Caterpillars can be bought from entomological suppliers but you may well be able to find some just by searching your garden. Caterpillars are delicate and some have hairs that can irritate your skin so try to avoid picking them up with your fingers. The best way to collect them is to break off the leaf or stem of the plant that they are on. Don't collect too many – two or three will be plenty.

YOU WILL NEED

- A bug box with a lid with air-holes, or a box/jar with muslin over the top

- Supplies of the right type of leaves for the caterpillars to eat (make sure you know what type of caterpillars they are, then you will know what to feed them – you can look online or in natural history books)

METHOD

1. Put caterpillars in the box.

2. Feed regularly.

3. Watch them spin a cocoon.

4. Check your box or jar regularly once the caterpillars have turned into cocoons; you will need to release the butterflies outside as soon as they emerge.

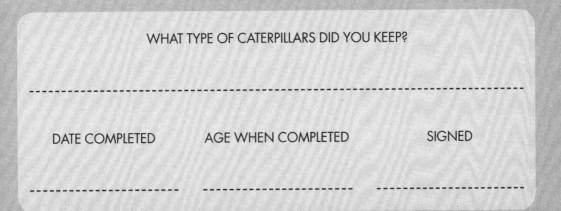

WHAT TYPE OF CATERPILLARS DID YOU KEEP?

DATE COMPLETED   AGE WHEN COMPLETED   SIGNED

-----------------------   -----------------------   -----------------------

No. 77

Blow Giant Bubbles

I'm sure you have blown bubbles before,
but have you ever made <u>really big</u> bubbles?
No? Try this method to create giant bubbles.

YOU WILL NEED

- 6 cups of water

- ½ cup of concentrated washing-up detergent

- ½ cup of cornflour

- 1 large spoonful of baking powder

- 1 large spoonful of glycerine

METHOD

1. Put the water in a large bowl or bucket.

2. Mix the cornflour in first, then stir everything else in thoroughly.

3. Leave it to sit for two hours so that everything mixes properly.

4. While you are doing that, use an old wire coathanger to make a massive bubble wand.

5. Dip the wand in the mixture and wave it firmly through the air to make bubbles. (Blowing won't work unless you have <u>huge</u> lungs.)

DATE COMPLETED   AGE WHEN COMPLETED   SIGNED

------------------------   ------------------------   ------------------------

No. 78

Make a Vinegar and Baking Soda Rocket

This one is quite dangerous. Be careful.

YOU WILL NEED

- Safety goggles
- Baking soda
- Vinegar
- Plastic water bottle
- Paper nose cone
- Cork
- Three pencils or sticks
- Sticky tape
- Tissue paper
- A large open space
- A responsible adult to supervise

METHOD

1. Check the cork fits the mouth of the bottle. It needs to be quite a tight fit.

2. Tape the pencils around the bottle neck so that you can stand it upside down.

3. Make a nose cone out of paper and stick it to the bottom of the bottle.

4. Put a couple of spoonfuls of baking powder into the centre of a piece of tissue paper and fold it up into a packet. This makes your slow-release fuse.

5. Pour vinegar into the bottle until it is a third full.

6. Put the baking powder parcel into the bottle.

7. Add the cork.

8. Shake.

9. Stand the rocket up on the pencils.

10. Run away.

WHY DOES IT WORK?

The baking soda causes carbon dioxide to build up in the bottle. When the pressure gets too great, it forces the cork out of the bottle and the pressure of the escaping gas creates thrust. The thrust makes the rocket leap into the air.

DATE COMPLETED   AGE WHEN COMPLETED   SIGNED

------------------------   ------------------------   ------------------------

No. 79

Go Pond Dipping

Ponds provide a home for a wide variety of insects, fish and amphibians. You'll be amazed at what you can find with just a few sweeps of your net.

YOU WILL NEED

- A net

- A bucket or tray to put whatever you find in

- Boots (the edges of ponds tend to be muddy)

METHOD

1. If you don't have a net, then make your own out of a wire coat hanger, a bean pole and an old stocking.

2. Find a pond.

3. Fill your tray with pond water.

4. Gently drag your net through the water. Be careful not to destroy any plants and try not to stir up the bottom too much.

5. Carefully tip the contents of your net into a tray and see what you have caught.

6. Put everything back in the pond when you have finished.

HANDY HINT

Try sweeping your net in a figure-of-eight motion through the water as this can catch more than just using a back and forth motion.

DATE COMPLETED   AGE WHEN COMPLETED   SIGNED

------------------------   ------------------------   ------------------------

You'll almost certainly get wet doing this so make sure you are wearing old clothes.

YOU WILL NEED

- A sunny day
- A hosepipe

METHOD

1. Attach the hosepipe to a tap and turn it on.

2. Experiment and try to work out where the water needs to be in relation to the sun for rainbows to form.

WHY DOES IT WORK?

The water droplets act like mini-prisms and split the white light into its different wavelengths. This creates the rainbow colours.

WHAT ORDER ARE THE COLOURS IN THE RAINBOW?

DATE COMPLETED   AGE WHEN COMPLETED   SIGNED

-----------------------   -----------------------   -----------------------

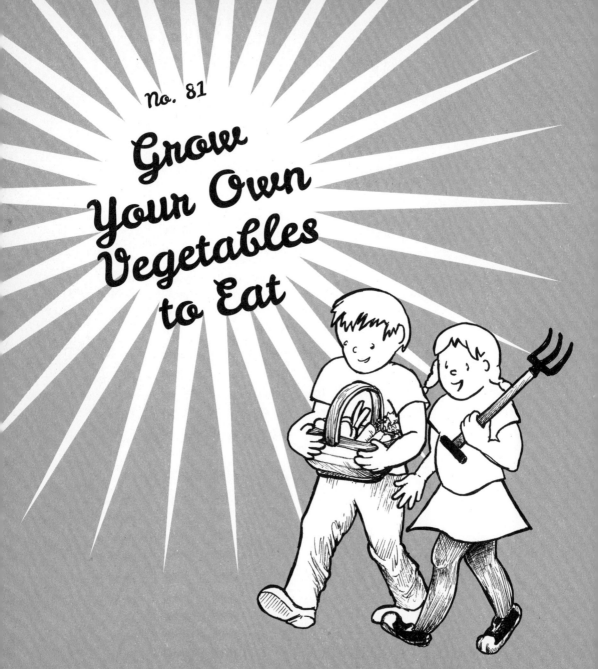

No. 81

Grow Your Own Vegetables to Eat

Eating vegetables that you have grown yourself is much more satisfying than eating bought ones. Start with something easy to grow, and work up to something more complicated.

YOU WILL NEED

- Seeds. Mustard cress is very easy to grow. Radishes are also easy. Tomatoes will do well provided you feed them (and dwarf varieties can be grown inside). Beans tend to get eaten by pigeons and slugs when young, but are very easy to take care of once they have got established. Carrots and parsnips can be a bit more temperamental, but are still worth the effort.

METHOD

1. Read the instructions on the packet! Different seeds need to be planted at different times.

2. Mustard cress seeds are very easy and can be grown on a damp piece of paper towel indoors.

3. Most other seeds need to be planted in potting compost or in finely raked soil.

4. Water your seeds regularly and use a watering can with a 'rose' head so that you don't wash the seeds away with a powerful jet of water.

THE VEGETABLES I GREW WERE

DATE COMPLETED   AGE WHEN COMPLETED   SIGNED

-----------------------   ------------------------   -----------------------

Make a Sundial and Mark the Time

Sundials are one of the earliest ways of marking the passing of time.
Ancient Greeks, Egyptians and Babylonians all had sundials.
Sometimes you will see basic sundials scratched on to buildings like churches.

YOU WILL NEED

- A stick

- A watch

- A sunny day

- Small stones or sticks

- Marker pen

METHOD

1. Put the stick in the ground in a position where it will get the sun all day.

2. Set an alarm to go off every hour. Go and see where the shadow falls at that point and put a small stone or stick marker in the ground to mark it. Write the hour on the stone/stick with the marker pen.

By the end of the day, you should have lots of little marker stones showing you where the shadow lands at different times of day. If you wanted, you could make a permanent sundial on a paving stone or out of a large piece of wood.

DATE COMPLETED   AGE WHEN COMPLETED   SIGNED

------------------------   ------------------------   ------------------------

No. 83

Germinate Fruit Pips

Avocado
stone

Sticks

Water level

Instead of just throwing away the core next time you eat an apple,
why not extract the pips and see if you can get them to grow?

YOU WILL NEED

- Apple seeds
- Paper towel
- Plastic box
- Fridge
- Pots
- Soil
- Avocado stone
- Long pins/cocktail sticks
- Jam jar

METHOD (APPLE SEEDS)

1. Extract the pips or seeds and dry them.

2. Place them between sheets of damp paper towel and put them in a sealable box.

3. Put them in the fridge for two months (to simulate winter).

4. Check them regularly to make sure the paper towel remains damp.

5. Wait until they have sprouted and then plant out into pots.

METHOD (AVOCADO STONE)

1. Extract the stone.

2. Stick 3–4 pins or sticks into the stone so that you can balance it across a jam jar (pointy end up).

3. Fill jar with water so that about 2cm of the stone is covered.

4. Put it in a warm place.

5. Check the water level regularly and keep it topped up.

6. It should start to sprout in 2–3 weeks.

DATE COMPLETED   AGE WHEN COMPLETED   SIGNED

-----------------------   -----------------------   -----------------------

Make a String Telephone

These were once commonly called 'lovers' telephones', presumably because couples could use them to whisper sweet nothings to each other, though it is possibly not the most romantic form of courtship.

YOU WILL NEED

- A long piece of string

- Two tins or similar. Golden syrup tins are excellent (and it gives you a good excuse to eat a lot of golden syrup). Pringles tins work well too. Plastic cups also work and are probably easiest, but don't look as good!

- Something to make holes with

METHOD

1. Make a hole in the centre of the base of each tin.

2. Poke the string through and tie a large knot at the end so that it cannot pull out.

3. Poke the other end of the string through the other tin and tie a knot.

4. Take a tin each, pull the string tight. One person speaks quietly into their tin and the other person listens at their end. It should sound as though the speaker is standing right next to them.

WHY DOES IT WORK?

Speaking into the tin causes the tin to vibrate and this vibration is passed down the string to the other tin. Sound waves can pass through the air too (which is why you can hear someone across the room speaking to you) but they pass through solids better. It is a bit like the difference between running on a nice bouncy running track (like the tight string) versus running on soft squidgy sand (the air). Less energy is lost, so it goes further. If you pluck the string while it is tight, you can feel how bouncy it is.

DATE COMPLETED   AGE WHEN COMPLETED   SIGNED

------------------------   ------------------------   ------------------------

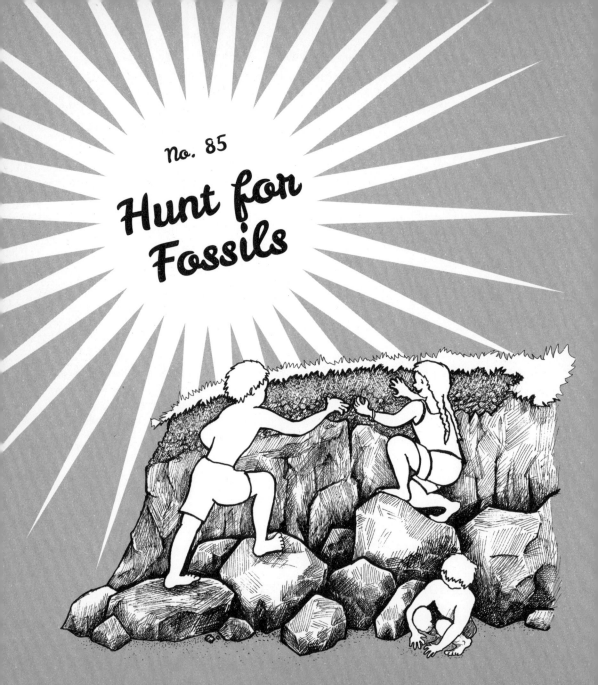

No. 85

Hunt for Fossils

Fossils form when a plant or animal dies in a place where its body won't be broken down by bacteria. Consequently, fossils tend to form on the seabed or the riverbed, where mud acts as a barrier to the bacteria. Over time, more layers of earth get deposited on top of the dead animal and the mud gets compressed and eventually becomes sedimentary rocks. The chemical composition of the animal or plant gradually changes and it becomes fossilised.

Not all rock has fossils in it, and some places are much better for fossil hunting than others. Seaside or estuary areas are often good and some places (like Whitby and Lyme Regis) are famous for their fossils. Usually, your best chance of finding fossils is to look in sedimentary rock like limestone.

YOU WILL NEED

- A place with the right geology for finding fossils

- A bag or box for your finds

METHOD

1. Hunt.

2. Sometimes you can try breaking soft stones open (drop them and shut your eyes) to see if there are any fossils inside.

I FOUND A

- -

DATE COMPLETED   AGE WHEN COMPLETED   SIGNED

- - - - - - - - - - - -   - - - - - - - - - - - -   - - - - - - - - - - - -

Dig an Archaeological Trench

Some gardens will contain more interesting archaeology than others. See what you can find in yours – but make sure you ask your parents' permission first; they won't be happy if you dig up their prize petunias.

YOU WILL NEED

- A spade
- A trowel
- An old tooth brush
- A sieve
- A finds tray (seed trays are good)
- Paper
- Pencil

METHOD

1. Choose where you want your trench to be and mark out the area.

2. If you are digging up the lawn (and only do that if you have permission!) lift up the grass carefully so that you can put it back afterwards.

3. Use the spade to take off the top soil and then use a trowel to dig your way carefully through the lower layers.

4. Use a toothbrush to carefully remove the dirt from any finds you make.

5. You can sieve the soil to locate even smaller finds.

6. Draw a plan of your trench and mark your finds on the plan so that you know exactly where you found each thing.

7. Try to identify all your finds afterwards. Your local museum can help.

You could use local history books or the Internet to try to find out the history of the area that you live in. Old maps will show you what towns and villages looked like decades ago and you will be able to work out whether your house is likely to be built on interesting archaeology or not.

DATE COMPLETED   AGE WHEN COMPLETED   SIGNED

------------------------   ------------------------   ------------------------

No. 87

Make a Lava 'Lamp'

Ok, so this isn't exactly a 'lamp', but it is nearly as impressive!

YOU WILL NEED

- A clear plastic bottle
- Vegetable oil
- Food colouring
- Water
- Fizz Alka-Seltzer tablets

METHOD

1. Fill the bottle a ¼ full of water.

2. Fill up the rest of the bottle with vegetable oil.

3. Add food colouring (it will mix with the water).

4. Chop up an Alka-Seltzer tablet and drop it into the bottle.

5. Watch the coloured bubbles rise and fall.

WHY DOES IT WORK?

Oil and water don't mix with each other, so the two liquids stay separate. Food colouring is water soluble, so it mixes with the water, but not the oil. The fizzy tablets release carbon dioxide and the light bubbles of gas attach to some of the coloured water, carrying it up to the top.

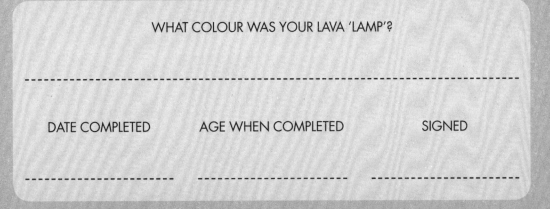

WHAT COLOUR WAS YOUR LAVA 'LAMP'?

DATE COMPLETED   AGE WHEN COMPLETED   SIGNED

----------------------   ----------------------   ----------------------

No. 88

Make a Mentos and Coke Water Spout

This is a messy one and definitely for outdoors.

YOU WILL NEED

- A bottle of coke
- A tube of Mentos mints
- An outdoor space

METHOD

1. Stand the bottle somewhere well away from anything that matters if it gets wet.

2. Drop five or six mints into the bottle.

3. Run away.

WHY DOES IT WORK?

Fizzy drinks have dissolved carbonic acid in them. This breaks down into bubbles of carbon dioxide and water. Bubbles form in a drink either around tiny dust particles in the liquid or on tiny scratches on the glass. This process is called nucleation. The more scratches, the more bubbles get formed. While Mentos mints look smooth, the sugar coating actually contains lots and lots of tiny bumps and scratches. This means that there are loads of places for bubbles to form. As the mints sink to the bottom of the coke, millions of bubbles form on the surface and then shoot to the top in an exciting and sticky geyser.

DATE COMPLETED   AGE WHEN COMPLETED   SIGNED

----------------------   -------------------------   ------------------------

no. 89
Bend Water Using Static Electricity

In 600 BC Thales of Miletus discovered that rubbing amber with fur made it pick up straw. History doesn't record why he was messing around with tree resin and bits of animal skin, but regardless of what he was trying to do, he had discovered static electricity; Yay for him! If you happen to have amber and fur lying around you could repeat his experiment. Alternatively, you can use a balloon to bend water.

YOU WILL NEED

- A balloon
- Running water

METHOD

1. Rub the balloon rapidly on a woolly jumper (or your own hair) to build up a static charge.

2. Turn a tap on slightly (you only want a gentle stream).

3. Place the balloon next to the stream of water and watch it deform the stream.

WHY DOES IT WORK?

Rubbing the balloon creates a negative charge. Water has a positive charge. Positive and negative charges attract, changing the flow of the water. You can also bend water using a plastic comb that you have run through your hair a few times.

DOES THE WATER BEND TOWARDS OR AWAY FROM THE BALLOON?

DATE COMPLETED   AGE WHEN COMPLETED   SIGNED

----------------------   ----------------------   ----------------------

no. 90

Egg Drop/ Egg Tower Challenge

This challenge requires that you make a parachute. Leonardo da Vinci drew a design for one in the fifteenth century and wrote that anyone using such a device 'will be able to throw himself down from any great height without suffering injury'. Da Vinci was far too sensible to actually try it out himself, but over the next few hundred years various foolhardy people jumped off towers or out of balloons with parachutes of various designs with mixed results. Nowadays, parachuting is so common that grannies do it to celebrate their eightieth birthdays. You don't need to make a parachute to support your weight (no really, DON'T), but you can test your engineering skills with a fragile egg instead.

A. Create a parachute/protective frame combo for the egg to enable it to survive being dropped out of a first-floor window.

B. Make a free-standing tower capable of supporting an egg at least a metre off the floor.

Good luck and if you don't want too much clearing up to do, you might want to hard boil the egg first.

YOU WILL NEED

- A box of plastic drinking straws

- Sticky tape

- Cardboard

- A light-weight scarf or a sheet of thin plastic (e.g. from a bin bag) to act as a parachute

METHOD

1. Before you make anything, plan your strategy.

2. If you are playing in competing teams, decide the rules and the time frame before you begin.

DID YOUR EGG SURVIVE THE DROP?   HOW TALL WAS YOUR TOWER?

-------------------------------------   -------------------------------------

DATE COMPLETED   AGE WHEN COMPLETED   SIGNED

-------------------------   -------------------------   -------------------------

No. 91

Build a Balloon Rocket

Most rockets need high-octane fuel to work but you can
build one that's propelled by nothing but air.

YOU WILL NEED

- A piece of thin string

- A balloon
  (ideally a long thin one)

- A balloon pump

- A drinking straw

- Sticky tape

METHOD

1. Cut the bendy bit off the straw and then thread the straw on to the string and check it moves freely.

2. Tie each end of the string to fixed objects and make sure that the string is tight.

3. Blow up the balloon and hold it while pinching the end shut tightly.

4. Tape the balloon to the straw.

5. Let go and watch the balloon shoot along the string.

6. Experiment with having the string at different angles. How steeply can the balloon climb?

WHY DOES IT WORK?

The balloon itself is elastic. By blowing up the balloon you have stretched the elastic and it wants to ping back. When you release the neck of the balloon, the balloon skin pings back into shape, forcing the air out of the neck of the balloon. The force of the expelled air creates thrust which keeps the balloon moving forward (the straw and the string are just there to steer it). The engines of a rocket work in a similar way. The rocket engine turns fuel into hot gas. This gas, like the air in a balloon, is forced out, pushing the rocket forward.

DATE COMPLETED   AGE WHEN COMPLETED   SIGNED

---------------------   ---------------------------   ------------------------

No. 92

Plant a Grass Head

These are very easy to make and you will end up with a face with grass for hair. You can then have great fun cutting the hair into entertaining hairstyles (which is better than styling a younger sibling or family pet).

YOU WILL NEED

- An old stocking
- An elastic band
- Grass seed
- A marker pen
- A pot
- Sawdust or soil

METHOD

1. Put some grass seed in the end of the stocking.

2. Put a few handfuls of soil or sawdust in on top.

3. Use the elastic band to securely hold the sawdust and grass seed in a tight ball.

4. Put the ball on top of the pot so that the grass seed is on top.

5. Draw a face using the marker pen.

6. Water, and wait for it to grow.

DATE COMPLETED   AGE WHEN COMPLETED   SIGNED

------------------------   ------------------------   ------------------------

No. 93

Make an Indicator and Test the pH of Things

Some substances are acidic (from the Latin *acere* meaning 'sour') and some are alkaline (from the Arabic *al-aqaliy* meaning 'burnt ashes'). It is quite fun to be able to test which is which and this challenge provides a way of using up cabbage without actually eating it. Red cabbage has been cultivated in England since the Middle Ages, so your medieval forebears could have done this experiment too, but as the pH scale wasn't invented until 1909, it is unlikely that they would have bothered.

YOU WILL NEED

- A red cabbage
- A knife
- A chopping board
- Water
- A saucepan
- Saucers
- Things to test

METHOD

1. Half fill a mug with water and then pour it into a saucepan.

2. Chop up the cabbage and put it in the saucepan.

3. Turn on the hob and heat up the mixture until the liquid turns purple.

4. Leave the mixture to cool.

5. Strain out the cabbage.

6. Put a teaspoon of lemon juice on a saucer and add a couple of drops of indicator. See what colour the mixture changes.

7. Try testing milk, vinegar, toothpaste, orange juice, water and baking soda.

RED	PURPLE	BLUE	GREEN
ACIDIC	SLIGHTLY ACIDIC	SLIGHTLY ALKALINE	ALKALINE

DATE COMPLETED   AGE WHEN COMPLETED   SIGNED

----------------------   --------------------------   ----------------------

no. 94

Make Your Own Compass

You could actually use this if you got lost in the woods. However, if you had a needle and a magnet with you, chances are you might have remembered the compass too! Still, it is good to have survival skills, even if you are unlikely to need to use them.

YOU WILL NEED

- A bar magnet
- A needle
- A bowl of water
- An old cork
- A knife
- A jam jar
- A piece of cotton
- A pencil

METHOD 1

1. Magnetise the needle by stroking it with a bar magnet, in the same direction, fifty times.

2. Cut a slice of cork.

3. Push the needle through the cork.

4. Float the cork on water.

METHOD 2

1. Magnetise the needle by stroking it with bar magnet, in the same direction, fifty times.

2. Tie the needle to a piece of cotton and adjust it so that it hangs level (fiddly!).

3. Tie the other end of the cotton around a pencil.

4. Put the pencil across the top of a jam jar so that the needle hangs inside the jar. This prevents the needle from being affected by a breeze.

Both needles should point north (or towards the magnet if you put it close to them).

WHY DOES IT WORK?

The iron in the needle contains lots of tiny 'magnetic domains'. However, these all point in different directions. Rubbing along the needle with the magnet makes these domains line up and gives the needle a magnetic charge.

DATE COMPLETED	AGE WHEN COMPLETED	SIGNED
-----------------------	-----------------------	-----------------------

No. 95

Build a Balloon Hovercraft

'Air-cushioned vehicles' or hovercraft were invented in the 1950s by Sir Christopher Cockerell who supposedly made the prototype out of a baked bean tin, a hair drier and a firework (CDs hadn't been invented yet). Unlike conventional vehicles, hovercraft don't have wheels; instead they skate along on a cushion of air which means they can travel over both water and solid land, as well as over quicksand and mud.

YOU WILL NEED

- An old CD

- The pop-up top from a water bottle

- A balloon

- Glue that will stick plastic

METHOD

1. Stick a piece of paper over the hole in the centre of the CD (otherwise the air will escape too fast). Use a pin to poke some small holes in the paper.

2. Glue the bottle lid to the centre of the CD. You could also tape it down with duct tape/electrical tape, but be careful not to cover the hole in the top.

3. Leave it to dry properly.

4. Blow up the balloon and put it over the bottle lid. If the bottle lid is popped down, the air won't escape.

5. Place the hovercraft on a flat surface and pop the bottle lid up.

6. Watch your hovercraft skate over the surface.

WHY DOES IT WORK?

Just like a real hovercraft, yours works because of the cushion of air between the CD and the table. As the surfaces are not touching, there is less friction and it is very easy for the craft to move. Try blowing gently on the balloon and see how little you need to blow to make it move.

DATE COMPLETED

AGE WHEN COMPLETED

SIGNED

no. 96

Make Fat Balls for the Birds

Bread isn't actually very good for birds. Make these tasty treats for them instead.

YOU WILL NEED

- Lard

- Bought bird seeds/
  currents/oats/flakes of
  cheese/unsweetened
  muesli

- A saucepan

- String

METHOD

1. You need twice as much of the dry ingredients as the lard.

2. Melt the lard on a low heat.

3. While it is melting, mix the dry ingredients together.

4. Stir the dry ingredients into the lard.

5. Form it into balls around the string. Be careful, it will be hot.

You can either make the balls by hand, or you can use a pot like a yoghurt pot or half a coconut shell as a mould. Make a hole in the top of your mould first, poke the string through and tie a knot. Then add the mixture and push it down well.

Hang up the balls in the garden and then settle down to birdwatch. Make a note of the different species you see (use a bird book to help you identify them).

WHAT BIRDS DID YOU SEE?

DATE COMPLETED   AGE WHEN COMPLETED   SIGNED

----------------------   ----------------------   ----------------------

No. 97

Make a Moth Trap

Moths are similar to butterflies, but many are nocturnal, so you rarely get a good view of them. However, they are easy to catch as they are attracted towards the light. One Christmas legend claims that a busy moth put off following the star to Bethlehem. By the time it was ready to go, the star had gone. Moths today seek out the light in the hope of finding the star and visiting baby Jesus. In China, moths have traditionally been associated with the spirit of dead ancestors visiting the living.

WHAT YOU NEED

- A light
- A large white sheet

METHOD

1. Hang up the sheet at dusk.
2. Place the light behind it.
3. Wait patiently.

WHY DOES IT WORK?

Moths navigate by flying at a constant angle to the moon (it is basically the moth equivalent to instructions like 'keep the river on your left'). This type of navigation is called 'transverse orientation' and works very well for moths when the moon is the biggest and most obvious light around. It works less well for them when there are other, brighter lights. So, you should feel sorry for the moths whilst you confuse them!

DATE COMPLETED	AGE WHEN COMPLETED	SIGNED
----------------------	----------------------	----------------------

No. 98

Go on a Night-Time Nature Hunt

Once you have fine-tuned your daytime tracking skills, it is time to try them out at night. Many animals are nocturnal, so if you go out at night, you will see different things. Badgers, rabbits, foxes and bats are often most active at dusk. Owls hunt at night and moths or even insects like glow-worms might be out.

YOU WILL NEED

Ideally, you would have night-vision goggles and infrared cameras, but given that you are unlikely to have those, you will have to make do with the following:

- A torch with a piece of red film or thin fabric stuck over the end (red light will disturb animals less)

- Sturdy shoes (you won't necessarily be able to see where you put your feet)

- Warm clothes

- A responsible adult

METHOD

1. You probably want to choose during the daytime where you are going to go. If you have spotted badger setts or fox holes during the day, then you could find a place nearby to hide just before dusk and sit quietly to see what comes out. Animals have very sensitive smell, so keep in mind that even if they can't see you, they might be able to smell you. Don't drench yourself in pretty-smelling bubble bath! If you can, find out which way the wind is blowing and sit down-wind of the sett (i.e. so that the wind blows from the sett to you, and not vice versa).

2. Try not to use the torch unless you have to. It is sensible to have one with you, but better not to use it.

You might hear more things than you see. Listen out for the screech of a barn owl hunting or the squeak of bats. Whilst you are outside, see what stars you can see. Sometimes you might see satellites passing overhead too. Hint: a 'star' moving rapidly across the sky in the same direction is not a star! Night-time navigation or night-time treasure hunts are good challenges to try too.

DATE COMPLETED   AGE WHEN COMPLETED   SIGNED

--------------------   --------------------------   ------------------------

No. 99

Watch the Sunrise

The ancient Egyptians used to believe that the sun died every night and was born again in the morning. One eighteenth-dynasty Pharaoh, Amenhotep IV (who was married to the beautiful Nefertiti) set off in a golden chariot to find the birth place of the 'aten' (sun). He discovered an area of the desert where there was a small break in the western line of the mountains, through which the sun appeared to rise. He named the place Akhetaten and built a holy city there. Sunrise and sunset were important to many ancient civilisations, and it is generally believed that Stonehenge was built along the alignment of the Solstice sunrise. If you wanted, you could build a temple or a city to the sun, but it is probably simpler just to get up in time to watch the sunrise.

YOU WILL NEED

- An alarm clock

- Warm clothes

METHOD

1. During the daytime, choose a spot where you can see the eastern horizon.

2. Find out what time sunrise occurs. In winter, it is later, which means you get more sleep. However, it is also colder, so you need more clothes.

3. Make a note of the exact time that the sun emerges.

IMPORTANT

If you value your eyesight, don't stare directly at the sun (even if you have sunglasses on).

DATE COMPLETED   AGE WHEN COMPLETED   SIGNED

-----------------------   -----------------------   -----------------------

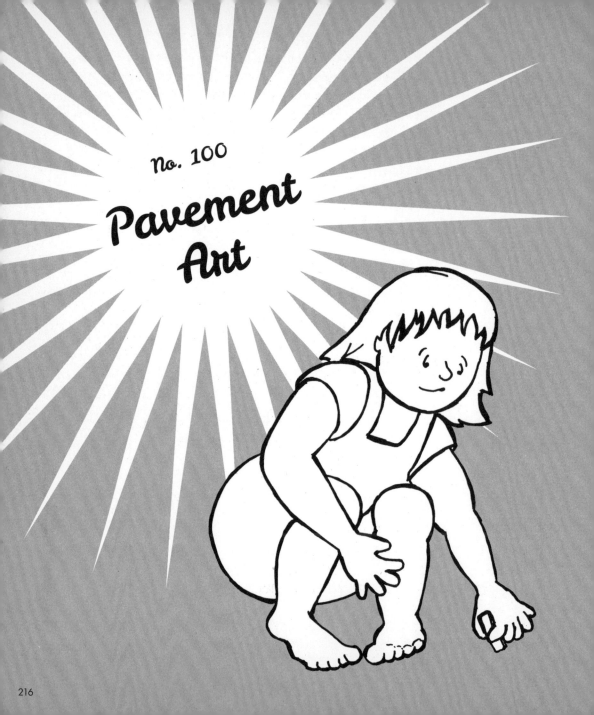

No. 100

Pavement Art

This form of artwork has been around for hundreds of years; pavement artists used to be referred to as *screevers*. Some pavement artists have great fun drawing optical illusions on the pavement. For example, they might paint a running river or a great big hole. This type of illusion is called *trompe-l'oeil* which means 'deceive the eye'. You could always make pavement art part of your garden sculpture trail.

YOU WILL NEED

- Pavement

- Chalks or pastels

- Permission of whoever owns that patio (chalk comes off eventually, but the marks may remain for a while)

METHOD

1. Get inspired and draw pictures on stone. You can rub out any mistakes and redraw.

WHAT DID YOU DRAW?

DATE COMPLETED   AGE WHEN COMPLETED   SIGNED

----------------------   ----------------------   ----------------------

No. 101

Make Elderflower Cordial

Elderflower has been used in cooking for centuries and was sometimes thought to have health properties. In fact, many people believed that the elder was magic; it could ward off witches and stop milk from going sour.

YOU WILL NEED

- A lot of sugar (2½kg)

- Water (1½ litres)

- Elderflowers

- 6 lemons or 2 lemons plus 85g of citric acid

- Container (for the elderflowers)

- Big pan

- Hob

- Sterilised bottles

- Muslin cloth or clean tea towel

- String

- Jug/funnel

METHOD

1. Collect the elderflowers. You will need about thirty large heads. Ask an intelligent adult to help so you are sure you're collecting the right plant.

2. Dissolve the sugar in the water on a low heat, stirring occasionally. Wait until you cannot see any grains of sugar left.

3. Rinse the elderflowers gently to remove any insects. Put the flowers in the sugar syrup, along with the juice from the lemons.

4. Cover and leave for twenty-four hours.

5. Take your clean muslin cloth and hang it up so that you can strain the syrup through it. An upturned stool with a corner of the cloth tied to each leg makes a good stand. Alternatively, you can just drape it over a colander, but you need to make sure it doesn't slip as you pour the syrup through.

6. Place a bowl under the cloth (a very important stage!).

7. Pour boiling water through the cloth to sterilise it. Discard the water and replace the bowl.

8. Pour the syrup slowly through the muslin.

9. Pour the strained syrup into the bottles.

DATE COMPLETED   AGE WHEN COMPLETED   SIGNED

------------------------   ------------------------   ------------------------

More
Challenges

Write some more challenges and give them to someone else to complete.
Think about things that you have done that you think other people would enjoy doing too.

Acknowledgements

I would like to thank my sister Elizabeth,
who has helped substantially with all stages
of this book, and Chris West for the hours
he has put into perfecting the design.

Visit our website and discover thousands of
other History Press books.

www.thehistorypress.co.uk

The History Press